The Insane ChatGPT Millionaire Guide

C Edmiston

Published by Internet Assets Ltd, 2023.

While every precaution has been taken in the preparation of this book, the publisher assumes no responsibility for errors or omissions, or for damages resulting from the use of the information contained herein.

THE INSANE CHATGPT MILLIONAIRE GUIDE

First edition. May 30, 2023.

Copyright © 2023 C Edmiston.

ISBN: 979-8223863670

Written by C Edmiston.

Table of Contents

Introduction

About the author

Introducing the author of the bestselling ChatGPT millionaire book,

C. Edmiston. An innovative tech enthusiast who dared to break the mould of a restrictive 9-5 work life! With over a decade of expertise in IT software development and website customization, the author boasts impressive credentials in computing. Many of which have taken years of testing and learning, and the author enjoys primarily working with WordPress, Python and C#, his preferred weapon of choice is Visual Studio.

By integrating ChatGPT and Open AI into his workflow, the author unlocked a treasure trove of productivity and completed more money-making projects than ever before. Captivated by the power of artificial intelligence and its potential to revolutionize our lives, he couldn't keep this secret to himself. And so, this trailblazing book was born, inviting you on an exhilarating journey to explore the limitless opportunities AI has to offer, transforming your life and income beyond your wildest dreams. So, get ready to step into the future and harness the power of technology like never before!

About you

Before diving into the dazzling world of AI-powered money-making, the reader should come equipped with a curious mind and a spirit of adventure! A basic understanding of computing and the internet will be a solid foundation, but don't worry; enthusiasm to learn and adapt is vital if you're not an expert. Plus, getting yourself a login on ChatGPT is highly recommended.

The book

With the author's extensive experience in computing, programming, and online money-making ventures, this book offers comprehensive and practical insights into leveraging AI to boost your income. The author's deep understanding of ChatGPT potential and everyday usage has been meticulously applied to every aspect of the book's creation. ChatGPT played an integral role in the development process, from the initial draft outline to proofreading and verification. The result is an invaluable resource that showcases the perfect harmony between human ingenuity and creativity alongside AI-powered assistance.

As you delve into the pages of this book, you'll discover how to harness the power of ChatGPT to maximize your earning potential. Each chapter has actionable strategies, detailed explanations, and real-world examples designed to help you master the art of using AI to your advantage. Whether you're a seasoned entrepreneur or a newcomer to online income generation, "The Insane ChatGPT Millionaire Guide" is a must-have guide that will transform your financial landscape. Embark on this thrilling adventure and learn how to capitalize on the limitless possibilities of AI, unlocking a world of prosperity and success like never before.

Get ready to unleash your inner techie, embrace the digital landscape, and embark on a thrilling, fun-filled journey that will transform your financial future. As you explore the cutting-edge techniques outlined in this book, you'll become an unstoppable force, harnessing the power of ChatGPT to catapult your income and ease of work life to stratospheric heights!

Chapter 1: Freelance Writing for Profit

Understanding the Freelance Writing Landscape

The Different Types of Freelance Writing

Numerous money-making opportunities for aspiring millionaires who can effectively harness the power of AI tools like ChatGPT to create high-quality content are now here. By understanding the various writing styles and formats while leveraging ChatGPT capabilities, you can cater to diverse industries and audiences, expanding your reach and income potential as a freelancer.

Blogging has become a powerful medium for businesses and individuals alike. Using ChatGPT to generate engaging and informative content can help you attract a wider audience, leading to increased revenue through advertising, affiliate marketing, and sponsored posts. These are just some content productions website owners are looking to employ freelancers for. ChatGPT can assist you in developing well-researched articles and generating fresh ideas, enabling you to focus on building your brand and scaling your freelance business to a great level.

If you are working on behalf of a client and want to understand exactly what ChatGPT can do for you, type "What are the top 10 trending topics in the wedding shoes industry?" to explore that niche on behalf of your client.

Although ChatGPT will help you immensely with this and be able to expand each topic for you, it will require proofreading and editing the draft article to your client's specifications. Rarely will ChatGPT do everything for you. Many bloggers are complaining that their sources for content are just using ChatGPT and nothing else. This is leaving many people criticizing those that use these tools. So don't let this be you. Use the tool, don't let it use you. It is good practice to use artificial intelligence to help you. However, remember that clients will undoubtedly use AI detection tools to check if an AI generates the work. Make it part of your freelance process to check your work on an AI detection tool before you submit it to the client.

You can find links to such tools in the resources section at the back of the book. If you are a freelance copywriter, ChatGPT prowess in crafting persuasive content can elevate your advertising, marketing, and sales campaigns for clients, leading to higher conversion rates and substantial profits. By leveraging ChatGPT ability to understand consumer psychology and write compelling, targeted messages, you can create persuasive materials such as website copy, product descriptions, email campaigns, and social media content that drive client results and income for you.

Request ChatGPT to create a compelling headline or call-to-action for a specific product or service. For example, you could ask, "What's a powerful headline for a sales page promoting a new fitness app?" or "Please write a call-to-action for an email campaign about a limited-time offer on noise-cancelling headphones."

Technical writing is a lucrative niche for freelancers, and utilizing ChatGPT to produce clear, concise, and accurate documentation can help you tap into the growing demand for skilled technical writers. ChatGPT can assist you in analyzing complex information, organizing it effectively, and translating it into easily digestible content.

Combining your technical expertise with ChatGPT AI-driven insights allows you to build a thriving technical writing business and generate a substantial income.

Ask, for example, "Please provide a step-by-step guide to setting up a home Wi-Fi network," or "How can I explain blockchain technology in layman's terms?"

Content writing is a broad and versatile category and, although like blogging, can be more related to shopping products and events rather than personal experience and opinion. Still, it is very lucrative for freelancers that know how to tap into the nuances of language. By harnessing ChatGPT capabilities, you can develop high-quality content across various formats and industries. ChatGPT can help you create engaging blog posts, articles, and more, streamlining your workflow and enabling you to take on more clients, boosting your earnings.

You could ask, "What are five engaging social media post ideas for a travel agency?" or "Please provide three unique angles for an article about remote work?"

As a forward-thinking business builder, staying informed of industry developments, and continuously improving your skills is crucial. Combining your writing talent with cutting-edge AI tools like ChatGPT allows you to stay ahead of the competition and build a thriving, lucrative freelance writing career.

Identifying Your Niche and Target Market

Finding your niche in freelance writing is crucial for standing out in a competitive market, attracting a loyal client base, and maximizing your profit potential as an ambitious, money-driven writer.

To identify your niche, consider your areas of expertise, interests, passions, and the industries and topics that resonate with you. It's important to consider your digital assets.

Then leverage ChatGPT to conduct thorough research on the demand for specific types of content and analyze the competition within each niche you know, helping you make informed decisions about which parts of these niches offer the most lucrative opportunities.

Ask ChatGPT for insights about the demand and competition in specific niches. For example, you could ask, "What are the most profitable niches in freelance writing?" or "What is the level of competition in the personal finance content market in [year]?"

Once you've determined your niche, pinpoint your target market by researching potential clients' demographics, preferences, and challenges. With ChatGPT assistance, you can gather valuable insights about your target market, allowing you to tailor your writing style and content to their needs and desires. In addition, you'll generate consistent work and drive your income upward by forging strong connections with clients who value your expertise. ChatGPT can also play a pivotal role in helping you refine your niche and target market over time. As you become more experienced and gain a better understanding of the content landscape, ChatGPT can help you identify emerging trends and opportunities, ensuring you stay ahead of the curve and adapt to the ever-evolving needs of your clients. ChatGPT can now browse the web for real-time category updates in certain niches.

You could ask, "What are the characteristics of the target audience for a health and wellness blog in December?" or "What are the main challenges businesses face in the travel industry when it comes to content creation?"

In addition to identifying your niche and target market, using ChatGPT to create high-quality, engaging content tailored to your audience will boost your reputation and credibility as a freelance writer. By consistently delivering exceptional work, you'll attract more clients, increase your rates, and ultimately increase your income.

The Significance of Content Marketing and SEO

Content marketing and SEO (Search Engine Optimization) are indispensable components of the digital landscape, playing a critical role in driving traffic, increasing brand visibility, and boosting business conversions. As a freelance writer with a money-making mindset, mastering these aspects can significantly enhance the value of your writing services and propel your income.

Content marketing involves creating and sharing valuable, relevant, and engaging content to attract and retain a target audience, ultimately leading to profitable customer actions. High-quality content helps businesses establish trust, authority, and credibility within their niche, making it a crucial aspect of their marketing strategy. By staying informed on the latest content marketing trends and best practices, you can create content that resonates with your client's target audience and drives results, positioning yourself as a sought-after writer in your niche.

You could ask, "What are the most effective content marketing strategies for a SaaS company?" or "How can a fitness blog use content marketing to increase user engagement and conversions?"

SEO optimizes your content and website structure to rank higher in search engine results, increase visibility, and attract organic, high-quality traffic. Understanding SEO principles, such as keyword research, on-page optimization, and link building, enables you to create content that performs well on search engines.

With the help of AI tools like ChatGPT, you can analyze keyword data and optimize your content to ensure it's both engaging and SEO-friendly, further boosting your client's online presence and reputation. Getting your client's site ranking with all the best resources is important, checkout the Ahrefs link https://app.ahrefs.com/ They allow you to setup client sites for free with just a simple process.

You could ask, "What are the key factors that influence search engine rankings?" or "How can I optimize my blog posts for better search engine visibility?"

Be aware that ChatGPT can now use the web to aid it in its queries so that this information may be constantly changed. For example, you could post your question and include the year and ask it to give you recommendations. This is how real-time capable the AI is of working with your requests.

A great SEO tip is to ask, "Visit [your website] and outline what SEO factors will create the greatest impact on my site?" or "How has the importance of voice search changed SEO practices in recent years?"

As an ambitious freelance writer, integrating content marketing and SEO expertise into your skillset opens doors to higher-paying clients seeking writers with a comprehensive understanding of digital marketing. You can easily offer a complete package that includes crafting compelling content, optimizing it for search engines, and aligning it with content marketing strategies. In addition, you'll be well-positioned to increase your rates and scale your writing career.

Utilizing ChatGPT for Content Creation

How ChatGPT Can Enhance Your Writing Process

ChatGPT is a powerful AI language model that can significantly enhance your writing process by acting as your confidential and hard-working creative partner, generating ideas, and providing writing support. By leveraging ChatGPT capabilities, freelance writers can overcome creativity issues, streamline their workflow, and produce high-quality content more efficiently, ultimately increasing their profitability and client satisfaction.

Writer's block is a common challenge for freelance writers, potentially slowing productivity and impeding the creative process. ChatGPT can help you break through this barrier by generating relevant ideas, prompts, and outlines based on your input, providing a starting point for your writing and sparking inspiration.

You could ask, "What are some interesting angles to explore for an article on remote work?" or "Can you suggest engaging blog post ideas about digital marketing trends?"

Streamlining Workflow: Time is money in freelance writing, and ChatGPT can help you optimize your workflow by automating certain tasks. It can generate outlines, draft sections of your content, or even suggest headlines, saving you time and effort. With AI assistance, you can focus on higher-level tasks, such as refining your writing or expanding your client base, leading to increased income.

Producing High-Quality Content: The quality of your writing is crucial to your reputation and success as a freelance writer. ChatGPT can elevate your content by suggesting phrasing, structure, and style.

It can also help with editing and proofreading, identifying errors and inconsistencies in your writing. Using ChatGPT AI-enhanced support, you can consistently deliver polished, high-quality content.

Ask ChatGPT to draft sections of your content or suggest headlines to save time and effort. For example, you could request it to "Please write an introduction to an article about the benefits of meditation" or "Suggest a catchy headline for a blog post on sustainable fashion."

Tailoring Content to SEO and Marketing Needs: Beyond its core writing capabilities, ChatGPT can help freelance writers meet their clients' SEO and marketing needs. By analyzing keyword data and optimizing content for search engines, you can ensure your work is engaging and SEO-friendly. This added value will make your services even more sought after and help you secure higher-paying projects. Although it's not quite as easy today as it used to be, with keyword density being almost irrelevant, you can ask ChatGPT to write more emphasis on the niche or topic you are writing about.

You could ask, "What are the most relevant keywords for an article on vegan diets?" or "Can you rewrite this article and put 10% more of the keyword [your keyword] in?"

You can take measurements of any changes you make and report them back to your SEO client, and if you give that much attention to detail, they will surely want to work with you again.

Generating Topic Ideas and Outlines with ChatGPT

Creating fresh and engaging topic ideas is crucial for freelance writers looking to make a substantial income and impress their clients. ChatGPT is a game-changer, transforming the idea generation process and helping you maximize your profit potential.

Efficient Topic Generation: Coming up with unique and captivating topics can be time-consuming, but with ChatGPT, you can streamline this process. ChatGPT will generate a list of potential topics tailored to your niche by providing a general theme or industry, saving time, and ensuring your content remains relevant and appealing to your target audience. This efficiency enables you to take on more projects and increase your earnings.

For instance, you could ask, "What are some interesting bullet point article topics on personal finance?" or "Can you provide engaging blog post ideas about sustainable living?"

Staying Ahead of Trends: As a freelance writer, staying updated with your niche's latest trends and developments is essential for success. ChatGPT AI capabilities allow it to analyze recent news, popular search queries, and social media trends, helping you create timely and engaging content. By producing content that resonates with current events and popular interests, you can attract more clients and secure higher-paying projects.

You could ask, "What are the latest trends in digital marketing?" or "What are people discussing on social media about [your trend]?"

Streamlined Outlining and Structuring: A detailed outline is crucial for producing well-organized and compelling content. ChatGPT simplifies this task by generating outlines based on your chosen topic, providing a clear structure to follow while writing. By breaking your content into sections and subheadings, you can maintain focus, ensure logical flow, and cover all essential points, ultimately leading to a higher-quality final product that attracts premium clients.

For example, you could request, "Please provide an outline for an article about the benefits of solar energy," or "Create an outline for a blog post on the top 10 travel destinations for holidays this year."

Client Satisfaction and Retention: consistently delivering fresh and engaging content is key to building a strong client base and securing repeat business. Using ChatGPT for topic generation and outlining, you can exceed your client's expectations and forge lasting professional relationships. Satisfied clients are more likely to refer you to others, further expanding your network and income potential.

Creating Engaging and High-Quality Content

Freelance writers aspiring to earn substantial income must consistently deliver engaging, high-quality content. ChatGPT is a valuable tool for achieving this goal, allowing you to create top-notch content that captivates your audience and sets you apart from the competition.

With ChatGPT assistance, you can elevate the quality of your work by providing a prompt or a few keywords related to your topic. This AI tool can generate relevant, informative, and well-written text that you can use as a foundation for your content. It helps you develop captivating headlines, write persuasive introductions, and craft compelling calls to action, ensuring your content captures your audience's attention and keeps them engaged.

For instance, you could ask, "What are some eye-catching headlines for an article about cryptocurrency investing?" or "Can you suggest engaging blog post titles about healthy meal planning?"

You can attract premium clients and secure higher-paying projects by consistently delivering engaging, high-quality content. Clients are willing to pay more for content that effectively resonates with their target audience and generates results. ChatGPT enables you to meet and exceed client expectations,

Boosting your reputation as a top-tier freelance writer. Remember to also look at the live listings in Google and the new Bard engine, as the target market for any client is always the audience of the World's biggest search engine! These will tell you what type of headlines others are using, and you can re-craft anything ChatGPT gives you, to be maybe 10% better than the rest.

Delivering engaging and high-quality content consistently is the key to maintaining client satisfaction and securing repeat business. Clients happy with your work are more likely to refer you to others, expanding your network and income potential.

Building a Strong Portfolio

Leveraging Ai to Build a Millionaire-Worthy Portfolio

Utilizing ChatGPT to build a strong and diverse writing portfolio can significantly increase your earning potential as a freelance writer. By leveraging AI's capabilities, you can create an impressive body of work that showcases your versatility and attracts high-paying clients.

ChatGPT lets you easily explore various niches, formats, and styles, even in areas with limited experience. ChatGPT can generate relevant and well-written content that you can use as a starting point for your portfolio samples by providing a prompt or a few keywords. This enables you to demonstrate your adaptability and range as a writer, appealing to a wider client base.

You could ask, "Write a sample blog post about eco-friendly travel tips," or "Create an excerpt for a case study on a successful marketing campaign in my [your niche] niche."

Showcasing Expertise: ChatGPT can help you create high-quality samples highlighting your expertise in specific areas. Incorporating AI-generated content in your portfolio can showcase your ability to deliver top-notch work in your niche. This increases your credibility and attracts clients looking for specialized writers, who often pay higher rates for their expertise.

For instance, you could ask, "Write an in-depth analysis of the impact of artificial intelligence on the job market," or "Explain the importance of cybersecurity for small businesses."

Some niches may come with nuanced keywords words that you can ask ChatGPT to summarize at the end of the article and include the most technical words possible in the article it writes for you.

Attracting High-Paying Clients: A strong and diverse portfolio is key to attracting high-paying clients who value quality and versatility. With ChatGPT assistance, you can create a body of work that showcases your skills and professionalism, making you an attractive choice for premium clients.

Using ChatGPT to Create Various Writing Samples

Embracing ChatGPT to create various writing samples. for your portfolio can unlock massive income potential as a freelance writer. By leveraging AI's capabilities, you can generate a wide range of samples that appeal to different clients and niches, setting yourself up for a steady stream of high-paying projects.

Diversifying Your Income Streams: ChatGPT enables you to create samples across numerous niches and formats, such as blog posts, copywriting, technical writing, and more. With a diverse portfolio, you can tap into multiple income streams, catering to clients with different needs and budgets. This diversification increases your financial stability and allows you to exploit lucrative opportunities.

You can ask, "What types of writing samples can ChatGPT help me create to strengthen my freelance writing portfolio?" or "How can I effectively use ChatGPT to generate high-quality content for different niches and formats?"

Outpacing Competitors: Using ChatGPT to generate high-quality writing samples quickly, you can position yourself ahead of competitors who may take longer to build their portfolios. This competitive edge increases your chances of securing projects, allowing you to rapidly grow your client base and income.

Impressing High-Paying Clients: ChatGPT-assisted writing samples showcase your expertise and versatility, making you an attractive choice for clients willing to pay top dollar for exceptional content. By catering to high-paying clients, you can boost your income and work towards your millionaire goals.

Minimizing Downtime: Utilizing ChatGPT to create various writing samples reduces the time spent on portfolio building, allowing you to focus on other aspects of your business, such as marketing, networking, and securing projects. By minimizing downtime, you can increase your overall productivity and income potential.

You can also ask, "What strategies can I use to attract high-paying clients using ChatGPT-generated writing samples?" or "How can I use ChatGPT to minimize downtime and increase productivity in my freelance writing business?"

Scaling Your Business: With ChatGPT support, you can produce diverse writing samples and secure a steady flow of projects. This influx of work creates opportunities to scale your freelance writing business, hire support staff, or outsource tasks, further increasing your income and propelling you towards your earning aspirations.

Accelerating Your Path to Wealth by Showcasing Your Work

Showcasing your work effectively using ChatGPT can accelerate your journey towards becoming a better freelance writer. By employing AI-powered assistance to create an impressive portfolio and following the tips below, you can attract high-paying clients and boost your income.

Maximizing Your Appeal: Use ChatGPT to generate well-crafted descriptions for your samples, making your portfolio more engaging and appealing to potential clients. A well-presented portfolio will pique the interest of clients with bigger budgets, helping you secure lucrative projects.

Enhancing Your Online Presence: ChatGPT can help you craft compelling copy for your portfolio website, including persuasive calls-to-action, unique value propositions, and impactful headlines. In addition, an effective online presence will attract more clients, increasing your chances of securing high-paying projects.

For example, you can ask ChatGPT, "Write a pitch for a potential client in the real estate industry, showcasing my experience in writing engaging property listings." or "Create a proposal for a healthcare company looking for blog content on mental health and wellness."

Leveraging Testimonials: Use ChatGPT to draft testimonial requests for satisfied clients, ensuring you gather persuasive and detailed reviews. These testimonials can reinforce your credibility and boost your appeal to potential clients, helping you command higher rates for your writing services.

You can ask, "Write a testimonial request email to a client I recently completed a project for, asking them to share their experience working with me on creating engaging blog content for their website." or "Write a testimonial request email to a client I recently completed a project for, asking them to share their experience working with me on creating engaging blog content for their website."

Marketing Your Freelance Writing Services

Establishing an Online Presence (e.g., Website, social media, LinkedIn)

ChatGPT can be an indispensable tool for marketing your freelance writing services and unlocking your creative and financial potential. By leveraging AI assistance, you can create a strong online presence and attract high-paying clients who value your skills above the rest of the mediocre marketplace.

Website Creation and Optimization: Use ChatGPT to generate engaging website copy, including persuasive headlines, compelling service descriptions, and powerful calls-to-action that can convert visitors into clients. ChatGPT can also help you optimize your website for search engines by suggesting relevant keywords and SEO-friendly content, boosting your visibility and driving more organic traffic.

Social Media Content: ChatGPT can assist you in creating captivating social media content, from attention-grabbing headlines to insightful blog post summaries. By sharing AI-generated, high-quality content on platforms like Twitter, Facebook, and Instagram, you can grow your audience, engage with potential clients, and establish yourself as an industry thought leader.

You can ask ChatGPT: "Help me create an attention-grabbing headline and concise summary for my latest blog post on content marketing trends to share on Twitter."

LinkedIn Profile Optimization: Use ChatGPT to craft an impressive LinkedIn profile, highlighting your expertise, accomplishments, and recommendations. ChatGPT can suggest powerful keywords and phrases that enhance your profile's visibility in search results, making it easier for high-paying clients to find and connect with you.

You can ask, "Provide suggestions on optimizing my LinkedIn profile to attract high-paying freelance writing clients in the [your niche] industry."

Generating Leads and Prospects: ChatGPT can help you identify and reach potential clients by generating personalized email templates and outreach messages. With AI-generated, targeted communication, you can increase your chances of securing high-paying projects and expanding your client base.

Try asking, "Generate a personalized email template for reaching out to potential clients in the healthcare niche, showcasing my expertise in medical writing." or "Identify a list of relevant industry conferences, events, or online forums where I can network with professionals and potential clients in the [your niche] niche."

Networking Strategies for Freelance Writers

Networking is vital to marketing your freelance writing services, as it helps you forge valuable connections and uncover new opportunities. Attend industry events, conferences, and workshops to meet other professionals and potential clients. Connect with other freelance writers and professionals in your industry, as they may be a source of referrals, collaborations, or valuable advice. Remember, nurturing your professional network can open doors to new clients and projects and enhance your credibility in the industry.

Ask ChatGPT this, "Help me find upcoming conferences or events related to freelance writing and digital marketing." or "Generate an engaging discussion topic for a content writing forum to showcase my expertise and attract potential clients."

Creating Persuasive Pitches and Proposals

Securing high-paying clients is crucial for making serious money as a freelance writer. Collaborating with ChatGPT to create persuasive pitches and proposals can dramatically increase your chances of winning lucrative projects and getting closer to that millionaire status.

Customized Pitches for High-Paying Clients: Use ChatGPT to generate tailored pitches targeting high-paying clients and demonstrating your expertise in their niche. By addressing their unique needs and showing a deep understanding of their industry, you can position yourself as the go-to writer for their projects and command top dollar for your services.

Ask ChatGPT to "Generate a tailored pitch for a high-paying client in the healthcare industry, showcasing my expertise in writing medical articles and blogs." or "Write me a pitch that includes positive hypnotic buying words throughout."

Outperforming the Competition: ChatGPT can help you stand out from the competition by crafting pitches and proposals that are engaging, polished, and persuasive. With AI at your fingertips, you can create content highlighting your unique value proposition and convincing potential clients to choose you over other freelance writers.

To help with this, ask, "Help me create a persuasive proposal for a content marketing project, focusing on my unique value proposition and previous successful campaigns."

You can tell ChatGPT your previous campaigns, and it will consider those and give you an even more accurate representation for this prompt.

Streamlining the Pitching Process: Time is money, and you can save both by leveraging ChatGPT capabilities. ChatGPT can speed up the pitching process, generating multiple high-quality pitches in a fraction of the time it would take you to write them manually.

Once you have a pitch draft, paste it into ChatGPT and ask, "Provide suggestions for improving my existing pitch template, making it more engaging and persuasive for high-paying clients in the [your niche] sector."

Expanding Your Client Base: ChatGPT ability to craft compelling proposals for various industries and niches allows you to expand your client base and tap into new markets. By reaching out to more high-paying clients and securing diverse projects, you can increase your income and pave the way to success for freelance writing.

Following Up with Prospects: Use ChatGPT to create personalized follow-up messages that keep you top-of-mind with potential clients. These well-crafted messages can help you stay on their radar and increase the likelihood of winning projects, contributing to your steady revenue growth.

By harnessing ChatGPT power in crafting persuasive pitches and proposals, you can boost the effectiveness of your marketing efforts, secure more high-paying clients, and move closer to achieving your independent freelance writing lifestyle and dreams.

Managing Your Freelance Writing Business

Setting Rates and Negotiating with Clients

Mastering the art of setting rates and negotiating with clients is crucial to becoming a highly successful and profitable freelance writer. ChatGPT can be an invaluable tool in this aspect of your business, helping you make informed decisions and communicate effectively with clients to secure the income you deserve.

Want to use ChatGPT to get better rates? Ask, "Provide me with information on the current market rates for freelance writers in the tech industry, focusing on blog posts and whitepapers." or "Help me craft a persuasive message to a client explaining why my proposed rate is justified based on my experience and the value I bring to the project."

Maximizing Earnings with AI-Powered Rate Setting: Utilize ChatGPT to gather real-time market information and analyze the rates of other successful freelance writers in your niche. By quickly processing large volumes of data, ChatGPT can help you determine competitive rates that reflect the value of your work and expertise, maximizing your income potential.

Crafting Persuasive Negotiation Messages: Leverage ChatGPT language generation capabilities to craft persuasive and professional messages when negotiating with clients. By creating well-structured arguments highlighting your unique selling points, expertise, and the benefits of your services, ChatGPT can help you confidently negotiate your rates and secure higher-paying projects.

Efficient Rate Adjustments: As your experience and reputation grow, it's essential to adjust your rates accordingly. ChatGPT can assist in analyzing market trends and your evolving skillset, helping you determine when and how to increase your rates to keep up with your increasing value in the market.

Renegotiation required? Ask, "Suggest a tiered pricing structure for my content writing services, offering different service levels and value for various budgets."

Strategic Pricing Proposals: Use ChatGPT to generate strategic pricing proposals that appeal to a broader range of clients and increase your earning potential, including tiered pricing and package deals. You can cater to different budgets by offering various options while maximizing revenue.

Bolstering Your Negotiation Skills with AI: ChatGPT can also provide insights and tips on effective negotiation strategies, helping you improve your skills and become a more confident negotiator. By honing your negotiation abilities, you can consistently secure fair compensation for your work and boost your income.

By tapping into ChatGPT potential in setting rates and negotiating with clients, you can position yourself as a sought-after freelance writer who commands top dollar for their services. Embrace the power of AI to help you make strategic decisions, communicate persuasively, and elevate your freelance writing business to new heights of profitability, inching closer to that millionaire dream that most people only dream of, while you work towards.

Time Management and Productivity Tips

Mastering time management and productivity are essential for achieving success in your freelance writing business and reaching your goals and aspirations. With ChatGPT as your ally, you can streamline your workflow, improve your efficiency, and get more done in less time, paving the way for higher earnings.

Maximizing Your Efficiency with ChatGPT-Generated Plans: Utilize ChatGPT to create customized daily, weekly, and monthly plans that allocate time for writing, marketing, and administrative tasks. Incorporating AI-driven plans into your routine ensures you work strategically and efficiently, maximizing your income-generating potential.

You can ask, "Help me create a weekly plan to manage my time as a freelance writer, focusing on balancing writing, marketing, and administrative tasks." or give it a list of your priorities and ask, "What order would I prioritize to give me maximum productivity and profit?"

Streamlining Content Creation: ChatGPT ability to generate ideas, outlines, and complete drafts can significantly reduce the time spent on content creation. This allows you to take on more projects, meet tight deadlines, and maintain high-quality work, ultimately increasing your earnings as a freelance writer.

Automating Routine Tasks: Leverage ChatGPT to automate certain routine tasks, such as drafting emails, creating social media updates, or generating article summaries. By automating these tasks, you can save time and focus on more critical aspects of your business that contribute to your goal of hopefully being a millionaire one day.

Try asking, "Suggest ways to automate routine tasks, such as email drafting and social media updates, to save time in my freelance writing business."

AI-Driven Learning and Development: Use ChatGPT to access up-to-date resources on productivity and time management strategies. By staying informed on the latest tips and techniques, you can continuously improve your efficiency and maximize your work hours.

Optimizing Break Times with ChatGPT: ChatGPT can also help you make the most of your breaks by providing relaxation techniques, quick exercises, or creative prompts to recharge your mind. By incorporating effective break strategies into your routine, you can maintain your energy and creativity, ensuring your work quality remains top-notch and worthy of high compensation.

For help, you can ask, "Provide relaxation techniques or quick exercises that I can do during my break times to help me recharge and maintain my energy levels."

Harnessing the power of ChatGPT to enhance your time management and productivity strategies can lead to significant growth in your freelance writing business. By working smarter, not harder, you can take on more projects, deliver exceptional work, and reach your full income potential, inching closer to your inspirational aspirations.

Streamlining Your Workflow with ChatGPT Support

In the quest for freelance writing success, leveraging the power of ChatGPT to streamline your workflow can be a game-changer, putting you on the path to becoming a successful writer. Using ChatGPT to optimize various aspects of your writing business, you can increase efficiency, enhance productivity, and ultimately generate higher earnings.

Quick Idea Generation: Use ChatGPT to brainstorm ideas for your writing projects, saving time and effort in the research phase. With a wealth of ideas at your fingertips, you can focus on delivering outstanding content that appeals to your clients and their target audience, leading to increased demand for your services.

You can ask, "Generate a list of article ideas for a client in the technology niche that I can use to create engaging content." or "Help me draft an introductory paragraph for an article on 'The Benefits of Remote Work for Businesses."

Efficient Drafting: ChatGPT ability to create drafts in record time allows you to complete projects faster without sacrificing quality. This improved efficiency enables you to take on more projects and meet tight deadlines, which can result in higher income and a growing client base.

Effective Editing and Proofreading: Rely on ChatGPT to proofread and edit your work, ensuring it is polished and error-free. You can command higher rates by presenting professionally crafted content, boosting your earnings and reputation as a top-tier freelance writer.

Ask ChatGPT if it will "Proofread and edit the following paragraph to ensure it is polished and error-free: [Insert paragraph]"

Continued Education: Stay ahead of the competition by using ChatGPT to access the latest information, trends, and best practices in the freelance writing industry. This knowledge empowers you to adapt and innovate, keeping your services relevant and in demand.

You can ask, "Bring me up to date with the latest news and advancements in the area of [your niche]"

By embracing ChatGPT support in your freelance writing business, you can achieve a streamlined workflow that enables you to focus on delivering exceptional content and growing your client base. This optimized approach can boost earnings and propel you toward your free of worry aspirations.

Scaling Your Freelance Writing Career

Identifying Growth Opportunities and Expanding Your Skill Set

In pursuing a millionaire status, using ChatGPT to identify growth opportunities and expand your skill set can be instrumental in scaling your freelance writing career. By leveraging AI's capabilities, you can stay ahead of industry trends, acquire new skills, and maximize earning potential.

Stay Informed: ChatGPT can help you stay informed about the latest trends, niches, and developments in the freelance writing industry. By regularly discussing relevant topics and news with the AI, you can identify potential growth areas and adapt your services to meet the changing needs of your clients.

Try asking, "Provide me with the latest trends and niches in the freelance writing industry that I can explore to grow my business."

Skill Development: Use ChatGPT to find resources such as online courses, webinars, and workshops to expand your skill set. The AI can also provide information about industry conferences and networking events, enabling you to connect with fellow professionals and learn from their experiences.

You can ask, "Provide me with the latest trends and niches in the freelance writing industry that I can explore to grow my business."

Content Diversification: ChatGPT can support you in exploring new content formats and writing styles. By experimenting with different projects, you can discover new areas of interest and broaden your service offerings, leading to increased demand and higher earnings.

Research Assistance: Rely on ChatGPT to help you conduct thorough research on new topics, industries, or niches. This can improve your understanding of these areas and enable you to provide specialized services to a wider range of clients.

Adapting to Client Needs: ChatGPT can assist you in quickly understanding and adapting to the unique needs of various clients. By tailoring your services and communication style to each client, you can forge strong relationships, secure repeat business, and enhance your reputation as a versatile and dependable freelance writer.

Stay flexible and ask, "Assist me in adapting my writing style for a new project that requires a conversational tone and focuses on the [your niche] industry."

Using ChatGPT to identify growth opportunities and expand your skill set, you can stay ahead of the curve and capitalize on new avenues for success. This proactive approach can greatly enhance earning potential, driving you closer to achieving your millionaire aspirations.

Establishing Long-Term Client Relationships

Establishing long-term client relationships is key to achieving independent financial dreams, as a freelance writer. ChatGPT can provide valuable support in nurturing these relationships and ensuring a steady stream of projects, leading to increased earnings and growth opportunities.

Deliver High-Quality Work: Use ChatGPT to assist you in producing exceptional content that exceeds client expectations. The AI can help with brainstorming, outlining, drafting, and proofreading to ensure your work is polished and tailored to the client's needs.

Effective Communication: ChatGPT can help you craft professional and clear emails, proposals, and updates to keep clients informed throughout the project lifecycle. By maintaining open communication lines, you can promptly address any concerns or questions and demonstrate your attentiveness to their needs.

To achieve this, ask, "Help me craft a professional and clear email update to inform my client about the progress of their project."

Receptive to Feedback: When receiving feedback from clients, use ChatGPT to help you analyze their suggestions and integrate them effectively into your work. This can show clients that you value their input and are committed to delivering the best possible results.

To help with this feedback, ask, "Assist me in analyzing the feedback I received from a client and provide suggestions on how to incorporate their input effectively."

Going the Extra Mile: ChatGPT can help you identify additional services or support that may benefit your clients. By offering these value-added services, you can strengthen your relationship with clients and position yourself as an indispensable partner in their success.

To aid with this, ask, "What value-added services can I offer to my clients in the tech industry to strengthen our relationship and increase my earnings?"

Client Retention Strategies: Utilize ChatGPT to develop strategies for maintaining long-term client relationships. The AI can provide insights on client preferences, industry trends, and best practices for client retention, helping you create a personalized approach for each client.

Just ask, "Provide insights on client retention strategies specific to the healthcare industry, focusing on creating long-term partnerships."

By leveraging ChatGPT capabilities to support you in establishing long-term client relationships, you can ensure a steady flow of projects and referrals, significantly increasing your earnings.

Leveraging ChatGPT to Increase Efficiency and Output

Harnessing the power of ChatGPT can significantly boost your productivity, enabling you to take on more projects and accelerate your journey towards becoming a freelance writer that makes much dollars. Here's how ChatGPT can support you in various aspects of your business, leading to increased earnings and growth:

Accelerated Content Creation: ChatGPT can help you quickly generate ideas, create outlines, and draft content. Using AI to create first drafts or assist with brainstorming, you can produce more content in less time, allowing you to work on multiple projects concurrently and expand your client base.

To get more content quicker, ask, "Help me brainstorm ideas for a blog post on [your niche] trends for my client."

Improved Editing and Proofreading: ChatGPT can support you in refining your work, ensuring it's polished and error-free. This saves time on manual editing and guarantees that you consistently deliver high-quality work, leading to satisfied clients and repeat business.

To help with this, ask along with your article, "Proofread and suggest edits for my latest piece on [your niche] for my target clients]."

Enhanced Marketing Materials: Leverage ChatGPT to craft persuasive pitches, proposals, and marketing materials that captivate potential clients. With AI-generated copy, you can create compelling content that showcases your value, helping you land more lucrative projects.

Streamlined Client Communication: ChatGPT can assist in crafting professional and clear emails, updates, and feedback responses, enhancing your communication with clients. Efficient and effective communication fosters strong client relationships and contributes to a steady flow of projects.

Continuous Learning and Skill Development: Use ChatGPT to stay updated on industry trends and best practices. The AI can help you find resources, courses, and workshops to expand your skill set, ensuring you stay competitive in the ever-evolving freelance writing landscape.

Chapter 2: Chatbot Development and Monetization

Understanding Chatbots and Their Applications

What are chatbots, and how do they work?

Harnessing the capabilities of ChatGPT in chatbot development can open numerous opportunities for monetization and growth. As a versatile and powerful AI, ChatGPT can be employed to create highly engaging and useful chatbots for various industries and applications. Here are some ways to leverage ChatGPT in chatbot development to achieve your millionaire goals:

Custom Chatbot Development: Offer custom chatbot development services to businesses, helping them automate customer support, streamline sales processes, and enhance user engagement. With ChatGPT natural language processing capabilities, you can create chatbots that understand complex queries and deliver personalized experiences, making your services highly sought after.

Need ideas for your first lucrative chatbot? Ask, "Help me brainstorm ideas for a chatbot designed specifically for the e-commerce industry."

Niche Chatbots: Identify and target specific industries or niches where chatbots are in high demand. Develop specialized chatbots powered by ChatGPT for e-commerce, healthcare, finance, or education applications, and sell them as premium solutions to clients in these sectors.

If your niche is healthcare, ask, "Can you provide a list of the most critical features to include in a chatbot for the healthcare sector?" or "How can ChatGPT-powered chatbots be used to improve patient engagement and streamline healthcare workflows?"

Chatbot Templates and Add-ons: Create and sell pre-built chatbot templates or add-on features powered by ChatGPT, allowing businesses to easily implement AI-driven conversational agents into their existing platforms. Offer customization services to adapt these templates to clients' needs and requirements.

Chatbot Training and Consultation: Offer training and consultation services to help businesses optimize their chatbot performance using ChatGPT. To maximize the chatbot's effectiveness and value, teach clients to fine-tune their conversational agents, develop engaging scripts, and analyze user interactions.

You can easily ask, "Can you suggest strategies to analyze user interactions with chatbots to improve their performance?"

Subscription-Based Chatbot Services: Develop ChatGPT-powered chatbots and offer them as subscription-based services to clients, providing regular updates, maintenance, and improvements. This approach allows you to generate recurring revenue while ensuring your chatbots stay up-to-date and competitive.

By leveraging ChatGPT in chatbot development and monetization, you can capitalize on the growing demand for AI-driven conversational agents and create multiple revenue streams. In addition, you will need to pitch your hand into programming, as you will have to understand the use of the Open AI API.

Key industries and use cases for chatbots

To capitalize on the versatility and potential of chatbots powered by ChatGPT, consider focusing on key industries and use cases in high demand. You can maximize profits and edge closer to your business aspirations by developing tailored solutions for these industries. Here are some ways to monetize ChatGPT in specific sectors:

Customer Service: Develop ChatGPT-powered chatbots that excel in handling customer inquiries, providing instant support, and escalating complex issues to human agents. Offer these chatbots as a premium service to businesses seeking to improve customer experience, reduce support costs, and increase efficiency.

Ask ChatGPT, "How can I train ChatGPT to handle customer inquiries in the telecommunications industry?" or "Provide examples of common customer inquiries and responses in the context of the telecommunications sector to fine-tune the model's performance."

E-commerce: Create chatbots that assist online shoppers with personalized product recommendations, purchase assistance, and post-sales support. Leverage ChatGPT natural language understanding capabilities to make these interactions more engaging and offer these chatbots as a valuable tool for e-commerce businesses looking to increase sales and customer retention.

You can ask, "How can I leverage ChatGPT to provide personalized product recommendations based on customer preferences and browsing history?" or "Using collaborative filtering how can I use the last three purchases of my customer, to recommend another product to them?"

You can feed lists of products your customer has purchased through the chatbot from your e-commerce store via the Open AI API just as easily as typing it into the web prompt interface. However, it is automatic, and you can complete the task much faster.

Healthcare: Develop ChatGPT-driven chatbots that offer basic medical advice, symptom assessment, and appointment scheduling. Market these chatbots to medical facilities and healthcare providers to improve patient care, reduce wait times, and streamline administrative tasks.

You can ask, "What are the best practices for ensuring that a ChatGPT-driven chatbot provides reliable and accurate medical advice?"

Finance: Use ChatGPT to create chatbots that provide financial advice, portfolio management, and transactional support. Offer these AI-driven financial assistants to banks, investment firms, and financial advisors to enhance client services and stay competitive in the digital landscape.

Use ChatGPT to ask, "How can I develop a ChatGPT-powered chatbot capable of helping users with portfolio management and financial advice?" for ideas. (Go to Chapter 10 for more dedicated Stock Market investing ideas)

Education: Design chatbots that facilitate learning and provide personalized tutoring experiences. By harnessing ChatGPT language generation capabilities, these chatbots can offer customized study plans, quizzes, and learning resources. Market these solutions to educational institutions, online course providers, and individual learners seeking tailored educational support.

You can ask, "How can I create a tutoring chatbot using ChatGPT that understands students' learning styles and adapts its teaching methods accordingly?" or "Which language and stack should I use to create a custom learning portal for students if I am a new programmer?"

By focusing on specific industries and use cases, you can develop specialized ChatGPT-powered chatbots that cater to each sector's unique needs and challenges. This targeted approach increases the value of your offerings and positions you as an expert in these fields.

The Role of ChatGPT in chatbot development

Leveraging ChatGPT in chatbot development provides an excellent opportunity for monetization and achieving your ambitious financial goals. As a cutting-edge AI, ChatGPT allows you to create sophisticated, engaging chatbots that meet the demands of various industries. Here are some tips on monetizing ChatGPT in chatbot development with a creative mindset:

Subscription-based models: Offer your ChatGPT-powered chatbot services on a subscription basis, providing continuous updates, improvements, and support. By ensuring your chatbot remains up-to-date and relevant, you can secure long-term, recurring revenue from your clients.

You can ask ChatGPT, "What features should I include in my ChatGPT-powered chatbot to make it appealing for a subscription-based model in the [your niche] industry?" or "What Python function do I need to write to create a login page for my chatbot?"

Chatbot consulting: Utilize your expertise in ChatGPT and chatbot development to offer consulting services to businesses seeking to improve their existing chatbot solutions or implement new ones. As a chatbot consultant, you can charge premium fees for your specialized knowledge and experience.

For this, you can ask, "How can I leverage my expertise in ChatGPT to offer chatbot consulting services for businesses in the insurance sector?"

Licensing and partnerships: Establish licensing agreements or partnerships with other chatbot developers or technology companies interested in leveraging ChatGPT capabilities. By offering access to your ChatGPT-powered chatbot technology, you can generate additional revenue streams while expanding your reach in the market.

To help with this, you can ask, "Discuss various partnership or licensing models with ChatGPT and develop a compelling pitch to present my chatbot technology to potential partners."

It's important to understand that many of these options require programming knowledge. However, this can be obtained slowly and surely with ChatGPT prompts such as those mentioned. Feel free to ask the AI whatever part of a concept we discuss that you don't fully understand.

By taking advantage of these monetization strategies, you can harness the power of ChatGPT in chatbot development to fuel your millionaire ambitions. Stay focused on delivering high-quality, innovative solutions that cater to the unique needs of each industry, and your chatbot development and monetization endeavors will be well on their way to success.

Designing and Developing Your Chatbot

Identifying Your Chatbot's Purpose and Target Audience

Defining your chatbot's purpose and target audience is crucial for creating a chatbot that addresses specific needs and has high market demand. By leveraging ChatGPT capabilities, you can create tailored chatbot solutions that generate substantial revenue. Here's how you can monetize ChatGPT in this area with a financially independent digital nomad mindset:

By leveraging ChatGPT advanced AI technology, chatbot developers can offer highly specialized and premium chatbot solutions to meet the unique needs of various niches and target audiences. Developing specialized chatbots allows for the creation of unique solutions that cater to specific user needs and demands. This approach allows for the charging of premium prices and attracting high-value clients.

On the other hand, incorporating ChatGPT into your chatbot offers a premium, highly interactive user experience. Market these advanced chatbots to businesses looking for top-notch customer engagement and satisfaction. Premium pricing can be justified by customizing solutions to each client's requirements.

You can ask, "How can I enhance my chatbot with ChatGPT to provide a premium customer experience in the retail industry?" or "Write me the process outline for functions in PHP and JavaScript to create a chatbot plugin on my client's WordPress site [clients site]"

License your chatbot technology: License your ChatGPT-powered chatbot to businesses in your target market. This approach allows you to generate recurring revenue from licensing fees while controlling your technology and its applications.

Just ask, "How can I structure my ChatGPT chatbot licensing agreement to maximize revenue while protecting my intellectual property?" or ask, "Discuss various licensing models and intellectual property considerations with ChatGPT to identify the best approach for this business."

White label chatbot solutions allow businesses to implement chatbot technology without investing in extensive research and development. By offering white-label ChatGPT chatbot solutions, businesses can brand the chatbot as their own, allowing for business partnerships and generating revenue from multiple sources.

Creating a platform powered by ChatGPT that other businesses can use for their specific needs is another approach to white-label chatbot development. This strategy offers a scalable and cost-effective solution for companies looking to implement chatbot technology. However, it requires some programming experience.

Both approaches to white label chatbot development allow businesses to harness the power of ChatGPT technology while building their brand and generating revenue. This can result in successful chatbot development and growth for the business.

Ask, "What features should I include in a white-label ChatGPT chatbot solution for the automotive industry?" or "tell me the steps I need to take to program a white-label chatbot solution for the [your niche] industry."

Affiliate and referral partnerships: Integrate affiliate or referral programs into your ChatGPT-powered chatbots. As your chatbot interacts with users, it can promote relevant products or services, generating additional revenue through commissions or referral fees.

You can ask, "How can I integrate an affiliate marketing program into my ChatGPT-powered chatbot for the fitness industry?" or "Share examples of [your niche] related products and services with the model, and work together to generate affiliate marketing strategies for this chatbot."

Data-driven personalization: Use ChatGPT advanced language processing capabilities to analyze user interactions and provide personalized experiences for your target audience. By offering highly tailored solutions, you can justify higher pricing for your chatbots and increase user satisfaction.

Consultancy and training services are an excellent way to help businesses implement ChatGPT-powered chatbots. By offering your expertise and insights, you can assist businesses in designing, developing, and deploying effective chatbots for their target audience. This service can generate additional revenue and position you as an industry expert, offering a valuable resource to businesses looking to improve their chatbot solutions.

Sharing your knowledge of ChatGPT and chatbot development through training sessions, workshops, or online courses is another way to position yourself as an industry expert. By educating others on building effective chatbots using ChatGPT, you can charge premium fees for your expertise and knowledge, providing value to those looking to improve their chatbot development skills.

By focusing on your chatbot's purpose and target audience, and leveraging ChatGPT to create highly specialized solutions, you can build a profitable chatbot development business. Stay informed about the latest trends and user expectations, and continually refine your offerings to maintain a competitive edge in the market, bringing you closer to your financial aspirations.

Crafting Conversational Flows and User Experiences

When designing engaging conversational flows and user experiences, ChatGPT can be an asset in creating chatbots that resonate with users and generate substantial revenue.

ChatGPT provides a powerful tool for developing chatbots with engaging conversational flows that deliver better outcomes. Here's how you can use ChatGPT to create top-performing chatbots that generate substantial revenue:

Design Natural Conversations: ChatGPT advanced language capabilities allow you to create chatbots that can mimic human conversation seamlessly. This results in a more natural and intuitive chatbot experience for users.

Enhance Customer Engagement: Use ChatGPT language model to craft chatbot conversations that are engaging, informative, and relevant to your target audience. This approach can increase user engagement and drive higher customer satisfaction.

Just ask ChatGPT, "What techniques can I use with ChatGPT to design conversational flows that are more engaging for users?" or "How can I utilize ChatGPT to craft more natural language interactions for a chatbot in the travel industry?"

Optimize Conversational Flows: Use ChatGPT's advanced language capabilities to analyze and optimize conversational flows, ensuring each interaction is relevant and efficient. This results in a better user experience and can lead to higher customer satisfaction.

Implement Contextual Responses: Utilize ChatGPT's language model to create chatbots that can understand the context and respond accordingly. This approach can result in more meaningful conversations and improved customer engagement.

To take advantage of these capabilities, ask, "How can I use ChatGPT to create a chatbot that can understand the context and provide relevant responses for a travel agency?" or "What are the steps for integrating ChatGPT into a chatbot for a restaurant recommendation service?"

By leveraging ChatGPT's advanced language capabilities, you can create chatbots with engaging conversational flows that drive better outcomes. Continuously refine your offerings based on user feedback and industry trends to maintain a competitive edge and achieve your money-making aspirations.

Integrating ChatGPT for Natural Language Understanding and Processing

By integrating ChatGPT into your chatbot development process, you can create more sophisticated, engaging chatbot solutions that have the potential to generate substantial revenue. Here's how to leverage ChatGPT's natural language understanding and processing capabilities to make money as a wannabe millionaire:

Develop industry-specific chatbots: Use ChatGPT's advanced language understanding to create chatbots tailored for specific industries, such as healthcare, finance, or legal services. You can command premium prices for your specialized chatbot solutions by targeting niche markets.

Offer multilingual chatbots: Capitalize on ChatGPT's language capabilities to develop chatbots that support multiple languages. You can expand your target audience, reach global markets, and generate additional revenue streams by providing multilingual support.

To do this, you can ask, "How can I leverage ChatGPT's language capabilities to develop a chatbot that supports English, Spanish, and French for a global customer support system?" or "Explore some techniques for incorporating multiple languages into my chatbot with ChatGPT, focusing on maintaining accuracy and natural language understanding."

Provide chatbot optimization services: Use your expertise in ChatGPT integration to offer chatbot optimization services, helping clients improve their existing chatbots' natural language understanding and processing capabilities. This service can attract businesses looking to enhance customer experience and improve chatbot efficiency.

You can ask, "Collaborate with ChatGPT to assess conversational data and user interactions, identifying areas for improvement and optimization in the target chatbot."

Develop premium chatbot features: Leverage ChatGPT's advanced natural language processing capabilities to create premium chatbot features, such as sentiment analysis, contextual understanding, or advanced personalization. Offering these high-value features, you can charge a premium for your chatbot solutions.

Charge others for API usage: If you create a ChatGPT-powered chatbot platform, you can monetize it by charging developers for API usage. By providing a powerful and easy-to-integrate solution, you can attract developers who want to leverage ChatGPT's capabilities for their applications.

For API information, you can ask, "How can I create a pricing model for API usage that reflects the value of ChatGPT integration while remaining accessible to developers and businesses?" or "Discuss strategies for determining API usage pricing with ChatGPT, focusing on balancing revenue generation with market accessibility."

By harnessing ChatGPT's natural language understanding and processing strengths, you can create chatbot solutions that stand out in a competitive market. Continuously refine your offerings based on user feedback and industry trends to maintain your edge.

Chatbot Monetization Strategies

Offering Chatbot Development Services for Businesses

Leveraging ChatGPT in your chatbot development services can help you create outstanding chatbot solutions that can command premium prices, pushing you closer to your millionaire desires. Here's how to use ChatGPT to maximize your earnings when offering chatbot development services for businesses:

Speed up development time: ChatGPT can accelerate the chatbot development process by generating high-quality conversational responses quickly. Faster development times mean you can take on more clients and increase overall revenue. Several language model versions of ChatGPT can be more suited to simple responses and cost less. So even if you are on a budget, ChatGPT can be accessible.

You can ask, "How can I use ChatGPT to generate high-quality conversational responses for a customer support chatbot in the retail industry?" or "Collaborate with ChatGPT to develop industry-specific conversational flows and responses, speeding up your chatbot development process."

Cater to high-end clients: By integrating ChatGPT into your chatbot development services, you can create chatbots with advanced natural language understanding and processing capabilities. These sophisticated chatbots can attract high-end clients willing to pay premium prices for top-tier solutions.

Just ask, "How can I create a ChatGPT-powered chatbot for a luxury hotel that offers personalized recommendations and support for guests?"

Diversify your service offerings: Use ChatGPT to expand your range of chatbot services. For example, you can offer services like chatbot content generation, chatbot optimization, or consulting on AI-powered chatbot strategies. By diversifying your offerings, you can cater to a wider range of clients and increase your revenue streams.

Develop industry-specific expertise: Leverage ChatGPT's extensive knowledge base to create industry-specific chatbots that cater to niche markets, such as healthcare, finance, or legal services. You can charge premium rates for your specialized services by establishing yourself as an industry expert.

You just need to ask, "Explore techniques for generating industry-specific chatbot content with ChatGPT, focusing on maintaining accuracy and relevance."

Create a ChatGPT-powered chatbot platform: Develop a platform that integrates ChatGPT and offers it as a service to clients who want to create their chatbots without starting from scratch. This approach allows you to generate revenue through subscriptions or licensing fees.

Offer training and support: As an expert in ChatGPT-powered chatbot development, you can provide training and support services to clients. Teach them how to optimize their chatbots and maximize ChatGPT's capabilities, increasing your revenue potential.

To offer this, ask, "What are the key topics and concepts I should cover when providing ChatGPT-powered chatbot training and support services for clients?" or "Write me a template script to cold call clients about the benefit of my experience with ChatGPT, and outline the best technical aspects I can know."

By incorporating ChatGPT into your chatbot development services, you can create exceptional solutions that attract high-paying clients and set you on the path to achieving your millionaire goals. Stay updated with the latest AI and chatbot development advancements to maintain your competitive edge and grow your business.

Implementing Paid Subscription Models for Premium Chatbot Features

Leveraging ChatGPT to power your chatbot's premium features can greatly increase the perceived value of your paid subscription model, attracting more users and boosting your revenue. Here's how to use ChatGPT to make money like a real business owner with a paid subscription model for your chatbot:

Enhance Conversational Capabilities: Offer an upgraded chatbot experience with ChatGPT's advanced natural language processing and understanding. Users who subscribe to the premium plan can enjoy more accurate, contextually relevant, and human-like responses, setting your chatbot apart from competitors.

To achieve this, ask, "How can I use ChatGPT to improve the conversational capabilities of my chatbot for premium subscribers, ensuring more accurate and engaging responses?" or "How should I interface with the ChatGPT API to respond to the user request for which page to find downloads in the Python language?"

Personalized Recommendations: Use ChatGPT's ability to analyze user inputs and generate personalized recommendations in various domains, such as e-commerce, travel, or entertainment. Users will appreciate the tailored suggestions, encouraging them to opt for the paid subscription.

Just ask for this, "How can I leverage ChatGPT's natural language understanding to generate personalized product recommendations for my e-commerce chatbot's premium subscribers?"

Exclusive Content Generation: Offer premium subscribers access to ChatGPT-powered content generation features. These can include article summarization, personalized news feeds, or creative writing assistance, providing added value to justify the subscription cost.

To aid with this, ask, "Learn from ChatGPT about best practices for generating high-quality content and tailor those practices to create exclusive features for the premium subscribers."

Priority Support and Assistance: Reward premium subscribers with priority access to customer support or dedicated ChatGPT-powered assistance, ensuring their needs are met promptly and efficiently.

Ask, "What are some effective strategies for using ChatGPT to offer priority support and assistance to my chatbot's premium subscribers?"

Continuous Improvement: Regularly update and enhance your chatbot's premium features, utilizing the latest advancements in ChatGPT technology. This will keep your subscribers engaged, reduce churn, and promote. You can create a more effective and lucrative monetization model by long-term loyalty.

By incorporating ChatGPT into your chatbot's premium features, you can create and generate consistent revenue. Stay informed about the latest AI and ChatGPT technology developments to maintain your competitive edge and drive your chatbot business toward an amazing financial future.

Generating Revenue through Affiliate Marketing and Sponsored Content

Utilizing ChatGPT in your chatbot can significantly boost the effectiveness of your affiliate marketing and sponsored content monetization strategies, propelling you towards millionaire status. Here's how to leverage ChatGPT for maximum profit potential:

Contextual Recommendations: ChatGPT's natural language understanding enables your chatbot to analyze user inputs and provide highly relevant product or service recommendations. Your chatbot can increase conversion rates and boost your affiliate revenue by offering personalized, contextually appropriate suggestions.

Try asking, "How can I use ChatGPT's natural language understanding capabilities to provide contextually relevant products by producing high-quality content showcasing my chatbot's benefits and features or service recommendations in a chatbot focused on personal finance?"

Seamless Integration: Use ChatGPT's advanced language capabilities to weave affiliate links and sponsored content into your chatbot's conversations in a natural, unobtrusive manner. This approach can enhance user experience and minimize disruption while promoting the desired products or services. A great method is to post a viral product on Facebook and create a ChatGPT bot to respond to people that ask, "Where can I buy this?".

Ask, "How can I integrate affiliate links and sponsored content into my chatbot's conversations naturally and unobtrusively?" or "Program me a JavaScript bot outline to respond to people automatically on Facebook via the API."

Targeted Promotions: Leverage ChatGPT's ability to analyze user preferences, behavior, and demographics to deliver targeted promotions that resonate with your audience. By highlighting sponsored content and affiliate marketing efforts to your users' specific interests, you can implement and drive higher conversion rates.

Just ask, "How can I use ChatGPT to analyze user preferences, behavior, and demographics to deliver targeted promotions for my [your niche here] chatbot?"

Dynamic Conversations: Utilize ChatGPT's conversational prowess to engage users in interactive discussions about promoted products or services. By facilitating engaging, dynamic conversations, your chatbot can address user questions or concerns, building trust and increasing the likelihood of conversions.

Performance Analysis: Use ChatGPT to analyze your chatbot's performance in promoting affiliate products or sponsored content. Identify areas for improvement and adjust your strategies accordingly to optimize your monetization efforts and increase your earnings.

For this, you can ask, "How can I leverage ChatGPT to analyze my chatbot's performance in promoting affiliate products and sponsored content and identify areas for improvement?" or "How can I Evaluate user interactions and feedback and draw insights to optimize monetization strategies and maximize earnings."

Adaptability: Stay updated on the latest advancements in ChatGPT technology and adapt your chatbot accordingly. By keeping your chatbot at the forefront of AI capabilities, you'll maintain a competitive edge and continue to drive revenue through affiliate marketing and sponsored content.

By integrating ChatGPT into your chatbot's affiliate marketing and sponsored content strategies, you can create a more effective and lucrative monetization model. Stay informed about the latest AI and ChatGPT technology developments to ensure your chatbot remains a top-performing money-making machine.

Marketing and Promoting Your Chatbot

Establishing a Strong Online Presence for Your Chatbot

To maximize your chatbot's revenue potential as a millionaire building their future proof business, consider leveraging ChatGPT in your marketing and promotional efforts. Here's how ChatGPT can help you build a strong online presence and turn your chatbot into a money-making machine:

Content Creation: Use ChatGPT's advanced language generation capabilities to create engaging and informative content for your website, blog, and social media channels. You can attract more users and increase conversions by producing high-quality content showcasing your chatbot's benefits and features.

You can ask, "Can you create an outline for articles, blog posts, and social media updates that highlight this chatbot's unique selling points and demonstrate its value to potential users?"

Community Engagement: Use ChatGPT to interact with potential customers and existing users on social media platforms and forums. Respond to questions, address concerns, and provide valuable insights to establish your chatbot as an authoritative and trustworthy solution in your niche.

Personalized Email Marketing: Leverage ChatGPT's personalization capabilities to craft tailored email campaigns that resonate with your target audience. By sending personalized messages that highlight your chatbot's unique value propositions, you can increase open rates, click-through rates, and, ultimately, conversions.

Influencer Outreach: Use ChatGPT to help identify and reach out to influencers and thought leaders in your industry. Collaborate with them to promote your chatbot to their audience, expanding your reach and credibility.

For outreach help, ask, "How can I use ChatGPT to identify and connect with influencers and thought leaders in the fashion industry to promote my chatbot?"

Press Releases and Media Coverage: Employ ChatGPT to craft compelling press releases and pitch your chatbot to relevant media outlets. By securing media coverage, you can increase your chatbot's visibility and establish it as a leading solution in your market.

You can ask, "Craft attention-grabbing press releases outline and media pitches that showcase this chatbot's unique features and benefits."

Chatbot Integration on Partner Websites: Partner with websites or platforms that complement your chatbot's offerings. Use ChatGPT to create seamless and engaging interactions when your chatbot is integrated into their sites. This approach can broaden your user base and increase your chatbot's exposure.

By incorporating ChatGPT into your marketing and promotional strategy, you can create a powerful online presence that drives user engagement, conversions, and revenue. Stay ahead of the competition by continually exploring new and innovative ways to promote your chatbot and leverage ChatGPT's capabilities to maximize your earnings potential.

Networking and Collaborating with Industry Professionals

It's essential to utilize every available tool to maximize your chatbot's revenue potential. ChatGPT can significantly influence your networking and collaboration efforts with industry professionals. You can use ChatGPT to your advantage:

Building Relationships: Use ChatGPT to draft personalized and engaging messages when connecting with industry professionals on social media platforms or via email. By creating thoughtful, well-crafted messages, you can initiate meaningful conversations and build lasting relationships that benefit your chatbot business.

Just ask, "How can I use ChatGPT to create personalized messages for connecting with professionals in the [your niche] industry?" or "Draft unique, tailored messages that demonstrate genuine interest and respect for each professional's expertise, creating a strong foundation for future partnerships."

Generating Ideas for Collaborations: Leverage ChatGPT's capabilities to brainstorm innovative collaboration ideas that benefit your chatbot and your potential partners. By identifying mutually beneficial opportunities, you can forge strong partnerships that help promote your chatbot to new audiences and increase revenue potential.

You can ask, "How can I leverage ChatGPT to brainstorm collaboration ideas for my finance chatbot and industry experts?"

Crafting Compelling Guest Posts: Use ChatGPT to write high-quality guest blog posts on relevant industry websites. Share your expertise and insights to establish your chatbot as an industry leader, driving more traffic to your chatbot and potentially converting new users into paying customers.

Preparing Presentations and Pitches: Employ ChatGPT to create engaging and informative presentations or pitches for industry events and conferences. You can attract interest from potential partners, clients, and investors by showcasing your chatbot's unique value propositions and demonstrating its effectiveness.

Identifying Influencers and Thought Leaders: Use ChatGPT to analyze social media platforms and industry forums to identify key influencers and thought leaders. Reach them with personalized messages and propose collaboration opportunities that align with their interests and expertise.

For many industries, you can ask something like, "How can I use ChatGPT to identify key influencers and thought leaders in the [your niche] industry?"

Creating Joint Promotional Content: Collaborate with your industry partners and use ChatGPT to develop co-branded promotional content, such as webinars, podcasts, or social media campaigns. By working together, you can amplify your reach and tap into new user segments, driving more revenue for your chatbot business.

By leveraging ChatGPT in your networking and collaboration efforts, you can create a strong presence in your industry, establish valuable connections, and maximize your chatbot's revenue potential. As a up and coming millionaire, harnessing the power of ChatGPT can give you the edge you need to succeed in the competitive chatbot market.

Utilizing social media and Advertising to Reach Your Target Audience

Harnessing the power of ChatGPT for your social media and advertising efforts can help you reach your target audience and maximize your chatbot's revenue potential. Here's how you can use ChatGPT to elevate your marketing and promotion strategies:

Crafting Engaging Social Media Content: Use ChatGPT to generate creative and attention-grabbing social media content that showcases your chatbot's features and benefits. By posting compelling content, you can attract followers, engage with potential users, and convert them into paying customers.

You can ask, "What are some creative ways to showcase my chatbot's features on social media?" or "Can you provide me with two different social media post ideas that highlight my chatbot's features?"

Developing Targeted Advertising Copy: Leverage ChatGPT's advanced language models to create persuasive, targeted advertising copy that resonates with your desired audience. Optimize your ad campaigns with tailored messaging to increase click-through rates and drive more users to your chatbot.

Creating Viral Content: Utilize ChatGPT to brainstorm and develop viral content ideas that can capture the attention of your target audience and prompt them to share your chatbot with their networks. Viral content can exponentially increase your chatbot's reach and help you acquire new users without significant advertising costs.

You can easily ask, "What are some viral content ideas related to my chatbot that focuses on mental health and wellness?" or "Generate two concepts for viral content that promote my [your niche] chatbot and encourage user engagement."

Analyzing and Optimizing Advertising Performance: Employ ChatGPT to analyze your advertising data and generate insights on the most effective channels, ad formats, and targeting strategies. Use these insights to optimize your advertising campaigns, maximizing return on investment and driving increased revenue.

Engaging with Your Audience: Use ChatGPT to draft personalized and timely responses to comments, questions, and feedback on your social media platforms. Engaging with your audience and addressing their concerns can build trust and loyalty, encouraging users to try your chatbot and potentially subscribe to premium features.

Monitoring Trends and Competitors: Leverage ChatGPT to stay informed about industry trends, competitor strategies, and user preferences. Use this knowledge to refine your social media and advertising efforts, ensuring you remain relevant and appealing to your target audience.

Just ask ChatGPT, "What are some viral content ideas related to my chatbot that focuses on [your niche]?" or "Generate concepts for viral content that promote my mental health chatbot and encourage user engagement."

By incorporating ChatGPT into your social media and advertising strategies, you can create a more powerful and effective marketing plan that drives user engagement and increases revenue. As a soon to be millionaire, using ChatGPT to its fullest potential can give you a competitive edge and help you reach your financial goals in the chatbot industry.

Analyzing and Optimizing Your Chatbot

Monitoring User Engagement and Feedback

Utilizing ChatGPT in your chatbot's analysis and optimization can help unlock greater revenue potential. Here's how you can use ChatGPT to enhance your chatbot's performance:

Analyzing User Feedback: Use ChatGPT to process and analyze large volumes of user feedback, identifying common themes and sentiments. This insight will allow you to address recurring issues and implement improvements that directly address user needs and preferences, leading to higher satisfaction and potentially increased revenue.

Just ask, "How can I identify common themes and sentiments from user feedback about my chatbot?" or "Analyze this set of user feedback and provide two key insights to improve my chatbot's performance."

Identifying Opportunities for New Features: Leverage ChatGPT to uncover patterns or trends in user interactions that may suggest unmet needs or opportunities for additional features. By expanding your chatbot's capabilities based on user demand, you can attract more users and potentially generate additional income from premium features.

Optimizing Conversational Flows: Utilize ChatGPT to analyze your chatbot's conversational flows and identify areas for improvement. ChatGPT can help you refine your chatbot's dialogue to provide more engaging, relevant, and efficient interactions, leading to higher user satisfaction and retention.

To handle this, ask, "How can I improve the conversational flow of my chatbot to increase user satisfaction in the fitness industry?" or "Review this conversational flow and provide two recommendations for creating more engaging and efficient interactions."

Personalizing User Experiences: Employ ChatGPT to create personalized user experiences by incorporating user preferences, history, and context into your chatbot's responses. Personalization can increase engagement and user satisfaction, encouraging users to continue using your chatbot and potentially invest in premium features.

Continuous Improvement: Use ChatGPT to regularly analyze your chatbot's performance and identify areas for optimization. This ongoing process will ensure your chatbot remains competitive and relevant, maintaining user interest and driving revenue growth.

A/B Testing: Leverage ChatGPT to generate alternative responses or conversational flows for A/B testing. Analyze the results to determine which variations perform best and implement the winning options to optimize your chatbot's overall performance.

To aid with this, you can ask, "What alternative responses or conversational flows can I test to optimize my chatbot?" or "Generate two alternative responses to this user query for A/B testing and explain the rationale behind each variation."

By integrating ChatGPT into your chatbot analysis and optimization process, you can create a more powerful, engaging, and effective chatbot that delights users and drives revenue. Using ChatGPT to enhance your chatbot's performance as an aspiring millionaire can help you achieve your financial goals in the chatbot industry.

Implementing Regular Updates and Improvements

As many millionaires know already. Life is about leverage. Leveraging ChatGPT for regular updates and improvements can help maximize your chatbot's revenue potential. Here's how ChatGPT can play a pivotal role in your chatbot's ongoing enhancement:

Analyzing User Interactions: ChatGPT can be utilized to analyze user interactions, providing valuable insights into user behavior and preferences. By understanding your users better, you can make targeted updates to your chatbot to improve its appeal and effectiveness.

You can ask, "What are some insights from recent user interactions that can inform updates to my chatbot?" or "Analyze these user interactions and provide two suggestions for updating my chatbot to better address user needs."

Generating New Content: Use ChatGPT to generate fresh, engaging content for your chatbot's conversational flows. Regularly updating your chatbot with new information and conversation topics will keep users interested and coming back for more.

Enhancing Personalization: Utilize ChatGPT to improve your chatbot's personalization capabilities. By tailoring your chatbot's interactions to each user's preferences, you can increase user satisfaction and engagement, potentially leading to more users subscribing to premium features or making purchases through affiliate marketing and sponsored content.

You can ask ChatGPT, "How can I enhance the personalization of my chatbot's interactions?" or "Provide strategies for improving personalization in my chatbot to create more engaging user experiences."

Automating Improvements: ChatGPT can automate some aspects of chatbot updates and improvements. This can save time and resources, allowing you to focus on more strategic aspects of your chatbot business and drive revenue growth.

By incorporating ChatGPT into your regular updates and improvements process, you can create a chatbot that continuously evolves to meet user needs and remains competitive in the market.

This ongoing commitment to enhancement will help you build a more successful chatbot business and move closer to becoming a millionaire in the chatbot industry.

Leveraging ChatGPT to Enhance Your Chatbot's Conversational Capabilities

You can think big when you start leveraging ChatGPT to enhance your chatbot's conversational capabilities can open several monetization opportunities. Here's how you can capitalize on the improved conversational prowess of your chatbot to generate revenue:

Premium Subscriptions: With ChatGPT-powered conversational capabilities, your chatbot can provide a superior user experience. Offer premium subscriptions that grant users access to these enhanced features, generating recurring revenue.

For this, you can ask "What are some premium features I can offer in my ChatGPT-powered chatbot to generate recurring revenue?" or "Suggest two premium features that leverage ChatGPT's advanced conversational capabilities for my chatbot's subscription plan."

Industry-specific Solutions: Use ChatGPT to develop chatbots tailored to specific industries, like finance, healthcare, or e-commerce. By creating specialized solutions with advanced conversational abilities, you can command higher fees for your chatbot development services.

Consultation Services: Offer your expertise as a ChatGPT specialist to businesses seeking to improve their chatbots' conversational capabilities. Provide consultation services and training packages, charging clients for your knowledge and skills.

Just ask, "What consultation services can I offer as a ChatGPT specialist to businesses looking to improve their chatbots?" or "List two consultation services I can provide to clients seeking to enhance their chatbots using ChatGPT."

Scaling Your Chatbot Business: As ChatGPT enables your chatbot to handle more complex user interactions, you can scale your chatbot business by targeting larger clients or expanding into new markets. Increased market penetration can lead to higher revenues.

Licensing Your Chatbot Technology: With a ChatGPT-enhanced chatbot, your technology may become attractive to other businesses. License your chatbot technology or establish partnerships with companies interested in leveraging your chatbot's advanced conversational features.

You can easily ask, "What are some potential partnerships or licensing opportunities for my ChatGPT-enhanced chatbot technology?" or "Identify two types of businesses that might be interested in partnering with or licensing my chatbot technology."

Improved User Retention and Monetization: A chatbot powered by ChatGPT can lead to better user retention and engagement, which can result in higher conversion rates for affiliate marketing, sponsored content, or in-chat purchases.

Chatbot Training as a Service: Offer training and fine-tuning services for other chatbots using ChatGPT. Help clients improve their chatbots' conversational capabilities by leveraging your expertise and charging fees for your training services. By harnessing ChatGPT's power to enhance your chatbot's conversational capabilities, you can create new revenue streams and grow your chatbot business. Stay committed to innovation and continuously explore ways to capitalize on the improved performance and user experience offered by ChatGPT to achieve your goal of becoming a millionaire in the chatbot industry.

Chapter 3: Profitable Blogging with AI Assistance

Identifying Your Blog Niche and Target Audience

Selecting a Profitable Niche

Leveraging ChatGPT can help you identify a profitable niche for your blog, increasing your chances of success and paving the way to becoming a millionaire in the blogging world. Here's how you can use ChatGPT to find the perfect niche:

Idea Generation: Use ChatGPT to generate a list of potential niches based on your interests, passions, or areas of expertise. Input your preferences and let the AI assistant suggest various niche ideas for you to explore.

You can ask, "What are some engaging blog post ideas related to [your niche]?" or "Generate two blog post ideas that cater to my target audience in the [your niche] market."

Market Research: ChatGPT can assist you in conducting market research to analyze the competition, audience size, and monetization potential of each niche. By automating this process, you can quickly assess the viability of different niches and make informed decisions.

Just ask, "What are the best practices for conducting a competitive analysis, estimating audience size, and assessing monetization strategies for a new product in [your niche]." or "Please provide two methods to conduct market research for the [your niche] market using ChatGPT."

Audience Insights: Use ChatGPT to analyze social media platforms, forums, and other online communities to understand better the interests, pain points, and preferences of your target audience. This will help you select a niche that genuinely resonates with your readers.

Try asking, "How can ChatGPT help me analyze social media platforms and online communities to understand my target audience better?" or "Provide two ways ChatGPT can analyze social media and forums to gain insights into my target audience's preferences."

Keyword Research: ChatGPT can assist you in finding high-value, low-competition keywords related to your niche, giving you a better understanding of the search landscape and potential traffic opportunities.

To find out more, ask, "How can I use ChatGPT to find high-value, low-competition keywords for my niche?" or "Please demonstrate two approaches to discover high-value, low-competition keywords in the [your niche] market using ChatGPT."

Monetization Potential: Have ChatGPT research and suggest potential monetization strategies for each niche, such as affiliate programs, advertising networks, or digital product opportunities. This will help you gauge the revenue potential of your chosen niche.

By utilizing ChatGPT to find a profitable niche for your blog, you can capitalize on the AI assistant's capabilities to save time and make data-driven decisions. This approach will help you identify a niche with strong market potential, increasing your chances of building a successful, high-revenue blog as an apprentice millionaire.

Understanding Your Target Audience

Utilizing ChatGPT can be a game-changer for understanding your target audience and making money like a real millionaire. ChatGPT's natural language processing capabilities can help you gather insights from various online sources, such as forums, social media groups, and competitor blogs. By analyzing this data, ChatGPT can identify common questions, concerns, and trending topics relevant to your audience.

Just ask to help you, "Please provide two methods for using ChatGPT to uncover popular topics and concerns in the [your niche] community." or "What are some ways ChatGPT can help me create detailed audience personas based on the computer training industry?"

Additionally, ChatGPT can assist in creating detailed audience personas by generating demographic data, interests, pain points, and preferences based on the information you provide. This comprehensive understanding of your target audience will enable you to produce tailored content that resonates with your readers, fostering loyalty and increasing the likelihood of them sharing your blog with others.

You can easily ask, "Please provide two methods for using ChatGPT to uncover popular topics and concerns in the [your niche] community." or "What are some ways ChatGPT can help me create detailed audience personas based on the data I provide?"

Monetizing Your Audience Insights with ChatGPT

With the help of ChatGPT, you can create highly targeted content that directly addresses your audience's needs and interests. This targeted content increases the potential for higher user engagement, which can lead to more opportunities for monetization.

For example, you can leverage your audience insights to create sponsored content or promote affiliate products that are highly relevant to your readers, increasing conversion rates and boosting your earnings. Additionally, consistently producing content that appeals to your target audience can grow your blog's traffic, making it more attractive to advertisers.

You can ask, "How can ChatGPT help me identify the best-sponsored content opportunities based on my audience insights?" or "What are two ways I can use ChatGPT to create engaging sponsored content that resonates with my target audience in my [your niche] niche?"

In summary, ChatGPT can be pivotal in understanding your target audience and creating content that appeals to them. By leveraging its AI capabilities, you can monetize your blog more effectively and maximize your earning potential, putting you on the path to becoming a blogging extraordinaire.

Conducting Market Research and Analyzing Competitors

Utilizing ChatGPT's AI capabilities can give you a significant advantage in conducting market research and analyzing competitors to make money like a high paid blogger and business owner. ChatGPT can help you gather and process data from various online sources, such as competitor websites, industry reports, and social media channels, to identify trends and opportunities within your niche.

Just ask ChatGPT, "Can you provide a list of the top 10 competitors in the [your niche] lifestyle blog niche?" or "What are the latest trends and developments in bitcoin and blockchain?"

Providing ChatGPT with a list of your main competitors can analyze their content, website design, and marketing strategies, giving you insights into what works well and areas that can be improved. ChatGPT can also help identify gaps in competitors' content, allowing you to target underserved topics and differentiate your blog from the competition.

You can easily ask ChatGPT, "How can you help me analyze my competitors' content, website design, and marketing strategies to gain insights? This is their website [website address]" or "What are two methods for using ChatGPT to identify gaps in competitors' content and target underserved topics?"

In addition to analyzing competitors, ChatGPT can monitor industry trends and developments. This enables you to stay ahead of the curve and ensure your content remains relevant and engaging for your target audience. By staying informed of the latest trends, you can capitalize on emerging opportunities and position your blog as a thought leader within your niche.

Just ask, "How can I leverage ChatGPT to stay informed about the latest trends and developments in [your niche]?" or "What are two strategies for using ChatGPT to capitalize on emerging opportunities and position my blog as a thought leader?"

Armed with the insights gained through market research and competitor analysis, you can use ChatGPT to create high-quality content that addresses underserved topics and resonates with your target audience. This targeted content is more likely to generate higher user engagement, which can be monetized through various channels, such as sponsored content, affiliate marketing, or display advertising.

By leveraging ChatGPT's AI capabilities to conduct market research and analyze competitors, you can create a blog that stands out in your niche and captures the attention of your target audience. This will ultimately help you grow your blog's traffic and revenue, leading you to become a blogging millionaire.

Creating Engaging Content with ChatGPT's Help

Generating Blog Post Ideas and Topics Using ChatGPT

By utilizing ChatGPT to generate blog post ideas and topics, you can create engaging content that attracts and retains a loyal audience. As a trainee millionaire, it's essential to understand that high-quality, captivating content is the foundation of a profitable blog.

To help with this, just ask, "How can I utilize ChatGPT to create blog posts with a clear structure, including an engaging introduction, informative body, and persuasive conclusion?" or "What are two ways to use ChatGPT to improve the organization and flow of my blog content for better reader engagement?"

Using ChatGPT, you can not only generate interesting topics but also create well-structured, informative, and persuasive content that keeps readers coming back for more. This continuous stream of high-quality content will help you build trust with your audience, establish your blog as an authority in your niche, and ultimately lead to increased traffic, social shares, and backlinks.

You can try asking, "How can I use ChatGPT to produce high-quality content that helps establish my blog as an authority in my niche?" or "What are two methods for leveraging ChatGPT to create content that builds trust with my audience and encourages them to share my blog with others?"

Monetizing Engaging Content with ChatGPT

Once you have a steady flow of engaging content, there are numerous ways to monetize your blog and drive revenue. Some of the most popular monetization strategies include:

Display advertising: As your blog's traffic grows, you can earn money by displaying ads on your site through networks like Google AdSense or by partnering with brands directly.

You can quickly get ideas if you ask, "How can I use ChatGPT to optimize my blog's layout and content to increase ad revenue through display advertising?" or "What are two strategies for leveraging ChatGPT to identify the best-performing ad placements on a fitness blog?"

Affiliate marketing: Recommend products or services related to your niche and earn a commission for every sale through your unique referral link.

Sponsored content: Partner with brands to create sponsored blog posts that promote their products or services, while still providing valuable information to your readers.

Selling products or services: Create and sell your digital products, such as eBooks, online courses, or coaching services, related to your niche.

Ask, "How can I utilize ChatGPT to research and identify the most profitable affiliate programs related to my niche?" or "What are two methods for using ChatGPT to create engaging content that promotes affiliate products without appearing overly promotional?"

By using ChatGPT to create engaging content consistently, you can attract a larger audience and generate more revenue through these monetization strategies. This AI-powered approach to content creation can be a game-changer for your blogging journey, whatever niche or subject your choose, it will help you achieve your goal of becoming a millionaire blogger.

Crafting Compelling Headlines and Introductions

In the blogging world, capturing readers' attention is crucial for driving traffic and revenue. By utilizing ChatGPT to craft compelling headlines and introductions, you can significantly increase your blog's click-through rate, social shares, and overall engagement, all of which contribute to your goal of becoming a successful blogger. Higher engagement rates typically lead to better visibility on search engines and social media platforms, resulting in more traffic to your blog. Thinking like a millionaire, you can monetize this increased traffic through various strategies.

To help with this, ask, "How can I leverage ChatGPT to create captivating introductions that encourage readers to continue reading my blog posts?" or "What are two strategies for using ChatGPT to analyze popular blog introductions in my niche and apply the best practices to my content?"

Headlines play a crucial role in affecting conversions in affiliate ads because they're typically the first thing a prospective customer sees. Their effectiveness lies in their power to grab attention, pique curiosity, and provide a succinct summary of the product or service. A well-crafted headline can intrigue a potential customer enough to engage with the ad and possibly make a purchase, directly boosting conversion rates. Furthermore, headlines that incorporate SEO keywords can increase online visibility, attracting a larger audience, thereby increasing the probability of conversions.

Just ask, "How can I utilize ChatGPT to create persuasive headlines and introductions that encourage readers to engage with my affiliate-linked content?" or " What are some effective strategies for optimizing affiliate content on my blog in terms of SEO, content structure, and product selection, and how can ChatGPT assist in implementing these strategies?"

Sponsored content and headlines go hand in hand in shaping user perception and driving engagement. The headline of sponsored content serves as the deciding factor on whether a user will click to read more or ignore the content altogether. An effective headline can stimulate interest, create an emotional connection, or trigger curiosity, thereby compelling users to interact with the content. In the case of sponsored content, headlines need to be crafted even more carefully, as they need to blend promotional elements seamlessly with informative or entertaining aspects.

Ask ChatGPT, "How can I utilize ChatGPT to create persuasive headlines and introductions that encourage readers to engage with my affiliate-linked content?" or "What are two ways to use ChatGPT to analyze successful affiliate content in my niche and implement those strategies on my blog?"

Collaborating with ChatGPT to Produce High-Quality Content

ChatGPT can be an invaluable partner in creating well-researched, engaging, and informative blog content. By providing the AI with your chosen topic and a brief outline, ChatGPT can generate drafts for your blog posts, complete with relevant information, cohesive structure, and a conversational tone.

You can then edit and refine the generated content to ensure it aligns with your brand voice and meets your quality standards. By collaborating with ChatGPT, you'll save time on content creation and be able to focus on other crucial aspects of your blogging business, all while maintaining a consistent output of high-quality content for your audience.

Collaborating with ChatGPT to produce high-quality content offers several advantages for those looking to make money as a real business blogger would. By consistently delivering engaging and valuable content to your audience, you can establish yourself as an authority in your niche, opening various monetization opportunities.

Easily ask, "What are two effective methods to collaborate with ChatGPT to generate high-quality, well-researched content for my blog?" or "How can I ensure that the content generated by ChatGPT aligns with my brand voice and meets my quality standards?"

Paid memberships and premium content: With a reputation for delivering high-quality content, you can introduce paid membership options or sell premium content, such as e-books or online courses.

Ask Chat GPT "How can I leverage you to create exclusive, high-quality content to offer as part of a paid membership or premium content package in the [your niche] industry?" or "What are two techniques for using ChatGPT to analyze and implement successful premium content strategies in my niche, [your niche]?"

Consulting and speaking engagements: As an authority in your niche, you may be invited to offer consulting services or speak at industry events, generating additional income.

Optimizing Your Blog for Search Engines (SEO)

Conducting Keyword Research

Understanding the importance of keyword research is the key to unlocking the full potential of your blog and maximizing your revenue. As a millionaire would advise another millionaire in the making, it's crucial to emphasize the significance of this foundational SEO strategy. By identifying and integrating the right keywords into your blog posts, you'll improve your search engine visibility, driving organic traffic and increasing your earning potential.

To conduct effective keyword research, familiarize yourself with the available tools. Google Keyword Planner, Ahrefs, and SEMrush are popular options that provide valuable insights into search volume, competition, and related keywords. These tools enable you to pinpoint the terms and phrases your target audience uses when searching for content within your niche.

For this, ask, "How can I use ChatGPT to generate a list of potential long-tail keywords and content ideas based on [your keyword] or topics related to my niche?" or "What are two effective strategies for using ChatGPT to identify and analyze the most relevant keywords for my blog?"

Focusing on long-tail keywords is an essential tactic for maximizing your blog's SEO performance. These longer, more specific phrases typically have lower competition and higher conversion rates, making them particularly valuable for driving targeted traffic to your blog. By incorporating these long-tail keywords into your content, you'll be able to capture the attention of potential readers who are actively searching for the information you provide.

Discover the secrets with, "How can I use ChatGPT to discover high-converting long-tail keywords that are relevant to my blog's niche?" or "What are two techniques for using ChatGPT to generate content ideas based on long-tail keywords that can drive targeted traffic to my blog?"

To further enhance your keyword research, you can leverage ChatGPT's capabilities. By inputting seed keywords or topics related to your niche, ChatGPT can generate a list of potential long-tail keywords and content ideas. This AI-driven approach can help you uncover hidden opportunities and stay ahead of the competition.

Once you've identified the right keywords for your blog, it's essential to strategically incorporate them into your content. This includes integrating keywords into your titles, headings, meta descriptions, image alt tags, and throughout your blog posts. However, avoid keyword stuffing, as search engines may penalize your blog for overusing keywords, resulting in lower search rankings.

For this try, "How can ChatGPT help me strategically incorporate keywords into my blog's titles, headings, meta descriptions, image alt tags, and content without keyword stuffing?" or "Rewrite this article with SEO friendly keyword search engine intent about the car industry niche."

As a soon to be millionaire guiding another millionaire in this industry, it's important to recognize the value of staying informed about the latest SEO trends and best practices. Search engines are constantly updating their algorithms, and staying up to date will ensure your blog remains competitive and continues to generate significant revenue. By combining your keyword research expertise with the power of ChatGPT, you'll be well on your way to building a profitable blogging empire together.

Ask, "How can I use ChatGPT to stay informed about the latest SEO trends and best practices to ensure my blog remains competitive in search rankings?" or "What are two methods for using ChatGPT to monitor and analyze the SEO strategies of successful blogs in my niche, and how can I apply those insights to my blog?"

Implementing On-Page SEO Best Practices

On-page SEO is the secret sauce that turns an ordinary blog into a search engine magnet, drawing in readers and increasing your revenue potential. It's essential to emphasize the importance of on-page SEO and its role in optimizing your blog for search engine success.

Incorporating target keywords throughout your blog posts is a fundamental aspect of on-page SEO. By strategically placing these keywords in the title tag, URL, header tags, and within the content itself, you'll signal to search engines that your content is relevant and valuable to users searching for those terms. Remember, moderation is key; avoid keyword stuffing to prevent search engine penalties that could negatively impact your rankings.

Image optimization is another crucial element of on-page SEO. Using descriptive and keyword-rich alt tags for your images not only improves your search engine rankings but also enhances your content's accessibility. Properly optimized images can drive additional traffic to your blog from image search results, increasing earning potential. A handy website to optimize your images for the web first is https://tinypng.com/ Drag and drop your image, and then download the smaller, optimized version. Taking up less space on your hosting and costing you less in bandwidth.

You can quickly ask, "How can I use ChatGPT to generate descriptive and keyword-rich alt tags for my blog's images to improve my search engine rankings and accessibility?" or "What are two strategies for using ChatGPT to optimize images on my blog and drive additional traffic from image search results?"

Ensuring your website has a clear, logical structure and is easy to navigate is essential for user experience and optimization of search engines. A well-organized site helps search engines crawl and index your content more effectively while providing a positive user experience that encourages readers to explore your blog further.

In today's increasingly mobile world, having a mobile-friendly website is non-negotiable. With most users browsing the web on mobile devices, search engines prioritize mobile-friendly sites in their rankings. Ensuring your blog is responsive and optimized for various screen sizes will help you capture this valuable mobile audience and boost your search engine performance.

Just ask, "How can I use ChatGPT to optimize my blog's content for mobile devices and ensure a responsive design for various screen sizes?" or "What are two strategies for using ChatGPT to identify and implement mobile-friendly best practices that will boost my search engine performance?"

Leveraging ChatGPT's capabilities can further enhance your on-page SEO efforts. By providing the AI with your target keywords and desired topic, ChatGPT can generate high-quality content drafts that incorporate your keywords in a natural and contextually relevant manner. This helps streamline the content creation process and optimizes your blog posts for search engines.

Embracing on-page SEO best practices and harnessing the power of ChatGPT will position your blog for search engine success. By consistently implementing these strategies, you'll drive organic traffic to your blog, maximize your revenue, and secure your place among successful blogging millionaires.

Building Backlinks and Promoting Your Blog

Understanding the power of backlinks and effective blog promotion is essential, and possible the number one ranking factor, still after all these years. High-quality backlinks endorse your blog, signaling to search engines that your content is valuable and authoritative. By building backlinks and promoting your blog, you can skyrocket your search engine rankings and increase your blog's visibility, ultimately boosting your revenue.

Creating valuable, shareable content is the foundation for attracting organic backlinks. High-quality content that provides unique insights, answers common questions, or shares practical tips will naturally draw attention from other websites and bloggers in your niche. By leveraging ChatGPT's content creation capabilities, you can consistently produce engaging, informative content that positions your blog as a valuable resource worth linking to.

Just ask, "How can I use ChatGPT to consistently produce engaging, informative content that attracts organic backlinks and establishes my blog as a valuable resource?" or "What are two strategies for leveraging ChatGPT's content creation capabilities to generate unique insights? Answer common questions, or share practical tips worth linking to?"

Guest posting on reputable blogs within your niche is another effective strategy for building backlinks and promoting your blog. By providing well-crafted, valuable content for other websites, you can establish yourself as an authority in your niche and earn high-quality backlinks that improve your search engine rankings. ChatGPT can assist in generating topic ideas and content drafts for your guest posts, making it easier to pitch and secure guest posting opportunities.

Engaging in relevant online communities and forums allows you to interact with your target audience and share your expertise. By actively participating in discussions and offering helpful insights, you'll build your reputation and attract more visitors to your blog. Whenever appropriate, you can share links to your blog posts that provide further information on the topic, earning valuable backlinks and driving targeted traffic to your blog.

You can ask ChatGPT, "How can you assist me in identifying relevant online communities and forums where I can interact with my target audience of [your niche] and share my expertise?" or "What are two strategies for using ChatGPT to develop valuable insights that I can share in discussions, build my reputation, and attract more visitors to my blog?"

Social media promotion is another indispensable aspect of building backlinks and promoting your blog. Sharing your content on social media allows you to tap into a vast audience and increase your blog's reach. Encourage your followers to share your content with their networks, which can lead to additional backlinks and increased visibility.

Harnessing the power of ChatGPT and implementing these backlink-building and blog promotion strategies will set you on the path to success in search engines. If you're looking for your first million in this industry, your expertise and dedication to these techniques will help drive organic traffic, increase your blog's visibility, and ultimately secure your position among the ranks of successful blogging millionaires.

To help with this, ask, "How can I harness the power of ChatGPT to implement effective backlink-building and blog promotion strategies that drive organic traffic and boost my search engine rankings?" or "What are two ways to use ChatGPT to enhance my blog's visibility and secure my position among the ranks of successful blogging millionaires?"

Monetizing Your Blog through Advertising

Exploring Different Blog Monetization Methods

As an aspiring millionaire guiding another millionaire in the making would tell you, it's crucial to understand the potential of monetizing your blog through various methods. A well-executed monetization strategy can provide a steady income stream, allowing you to focus on growing your blog and sharing your expertise with your audience. In this guide, we'll explore how ChatGPT can be used to assist you in making money through advertising and other monetization methods.

Affiliate marketing is a popular and profitable way to monetize your blog. By partnering with companies and promoting their products or services, you can earn commissions for every sale or lead generated through your referral links. ChatGPT can be a valuable tool in your affiliate marketing efforts by helping you create persuasive product reviews, informative comparison articles, and engaging promotional content that encourages your readers to explore and purchase your recommended products.

Display advertising, such as banner ads and sponsored content, is another effective blog monetization method. By partnering with ad networks like Google AdSense, you can earn revenue based on ad impressions or clicks on your blog. ChatGPT can assist you in optimizing your blog content to increase page views and ad impressions, helping you make the most of your display advertising opportunities.

Sponsored content offers yet another avenue for monetizing your blog. By collaborating with brands to create content that promotes their products or services, you can earn revenue while maintaining control over the content on your blog. ChatGPT can help you craft compelling sponsored articles that align with your brand voice and resonate with your audience, making it an attractive option for you and the brands you partner with.

You can easily ask, "How can I leverage ChatGPT to craft compelling sponsored articles that align with my brand voice, resonate with my audience, and make my blog an attractive option for brands to partner with?" or "What are two methods for using ChatGPT to create high-quality sponsored content that promotes the products or services of the brands I collaborate with while maintaining control over my blog content?"

Selling digital products or services is another lucrative blog monetization method. Whether offering e-books, online courses, or consulting services, ChatGPT can be a valuable resource in creating high-quality, informative content that showcases your expertise and entices your audience to invest in your offerings.

Just ask, "How can I use ChatGPT to create high-quality, informative content that showcases my expertise and entices my audience to invest in my digital products or services, such as e-books, online courses, or consulting services?" or "What are two strategies for leveraging ChatGPT's capabilities to improve my digital product or service offerings and increase my earnings from these monetization methods?"

By harnessing the power of ChatGPT to assist with your blog monetization efforts, you can effectively implement various monetization methods and maximize your earning potential. As a millionaire giving another millionaire the best secrets in the industry would agree, your knowledge and strategic use of these monetization techniques will pave the way for success and continued growth in blogging.

Selecting the Most Suitable Monetization Strategy

Choosing the most suitable monetization strategy for your blog is a crucial decision that can significantly impact your income potential. It's essential to understand the nuances of different monetization strategies and how ChatGPT can help you capitalize on them.

To select the best monetization strategy for your blog, consider your audience's preferences and needs. Affiliate marketing can be highly effective if your audience is interested in learning about products or services within your niche. ChatGPT can help you create engaging product reviews, comparisons, and resource guides that seamlessly integrate affiliate links while providing genuine value to your readers.

Ask, "How can I use ChatGPT to generate a list of engaging topic ideas for creating affiliate marketing content like product reviews, comparisons, and resource guides that cater to my audience's preferences while seamlessly integrating affiliate links and generating revenue?"

Display advertising and sponsored content may be more suitable for blogs centered around informational or educational content. ChatGPT can assist you in crafting informative and engaging content that attracts a steady stream of visitors, increasing your ad impressions and clicks. AI can also help you create high-quality sponsored content that aligns with your brand and resonates with your audience, making your blog an attractive platform for potential sponsors.

When selecting a monetization strategy, it's essential to consider your blog's overall goals. Offering digital products or services might be ideal if you aim to establish yourself as an expert within your niche. ChatGPT can help you create compelling sales copy, in-depth e-books, or comprehensive online courses that showcase your expertise and entice your audience to invest in your offerings.

You can get a great response by asking, "How can I leverage ChatGPT to create compelling sales copy, in-depth e-books, or comprehensive online courses that showcase my expertise, cater to my audience's needs, and entice them to invest in my digital products or services?" or "What are two methods for using ChatGPT to develop and promote digital products or services that align with my blog's overall goals and maximize my earnings from this monetization method?"

It's crucial to emphasize the importance of experimenting with different monetization strategies to find the best combination for your blog. Diversifying your income sources maximizes your earning potential and reduces your reliance on any single revenue stream, providing financial stability and flexibility.

By leveraging ChatGPT's capabilities to create high-quality content tailored to your chosen monetization strategy, you'll be well on your way to building a profitable blog that paves the way for success and continued growth in the competitive blogging world.

Setting Up and Managing Ad Networks

Successfully setting up and managing ad networks is a crucial aspect of blog monetization that can significantly boost your earnings. As a entrepreneur guiding another millionaire in the making, understanding the ins and outs of ad networks and how ChatGPT can help you optimize your blog's advertising potential is essential.

Getting started with ad networks like Google AdSense is relatively straightforward. Sign up for the ad network of your choice and follow their guidelines for placing ads on your site. Remember that ad networks often have strict requirements regarding site content and quality, so ensure your blog meets these standards before applying.

Just ask ChatGPT, "How can I use ChatGPT to identify the most strategic ad placements on my blog to maximize visibility and revenue potential?" or "What examples of captivating content can ChatGPT generate to keep readers engaged and increase the likelihood of ad interaction?"

Once you've successfully joined an ad network, strategically place ads on your blog to maximize visibility and revenue potential. Use ChatGPT to create captivating content that keeps readers engaged, increasing the likelihood they'll interact with ads on your site. Moreover, ChatGPT can help you generate well-researched content that seamlessly incorporates sponsored products or services, making your affiliate marketing efforts feel authentic and relevant to your readers.

"What are the essential steps to set up Google AdSense or other ad networks on my blog, and how can I use ChatGPT to create content that meets their quality requirements?" or "How can ChatGPT help me generate content ideas that are engaging and compliant with ad network guidelines, ensuring a smooth approval process?"

Regularly monitoring your ad network's performance is crucial for optimizing your earnings. Monitor metrics like click-through rates (CTR), cost per click (CPC), and overall revenue. Use this data to make informed ad placements, formats, and sizes decisions. For example, you might discover that larger ad units placed within the content perform better than smaller ads in the sidebar.

You can ask, "What specific metrics should I monitor when assessing my ad network's performance, and how can ChatGPT help me interpret these metrics to optimize my earnings?" or "How can I use ChatGPT to determine the most effective ad formats and sizes for my blog based on my ad network's performance data?"

It's essential to encourage experimentation and continuous improvement. Test different ad placements and formats to determine which combinations yield the best results for your blog. Additionally, consider diversifying your ad networks to tap into different audiences and revenue streams. If you are using Google AdSense however, you can set them to be auto ads, which means they will optimize based on Googles own data. This is normally the most optimal, but you maybe prefer your own layout of ads.

Just ask, "How can ChatGPT guide testing different ad placements and formats to find the most effective combinations for my blog?" or "What advice can ChatGPT offer on diversifying my ad networks to reach different audiences and revenue streams, ensuring long-term financial success?"

By leveraging ChatGPT's content creation capabilities and effectively managing your ad network, you can maximize your blog's monetization potential through advertising and affiliate marketing. This powerful combination will set you on the path to financial success and help you join the ranks of entrepreneurs who have turned their passion for blogging into a lucrative business.

Growing Your Blog's Traffic and Audience

Developing a Content Marketing Strategy

Developing a content marketing strategy is crucial in growing your blog's traffic and audience. It's essential to understand how ChatGPT can help you devise a data-driven and targeted content marketing plan tailored to your blog's niche and audience.

First and foremost, ChatGPT can assist you in identifying trending topics within your niche. By staying up to date on current trends and addressing them in your content, you'll ensure that your blog remains relevant and engaging to your target audience. This strategy boosts traffic and increases the likelihood of your content being shared on social media, further expanding your reach.

You can easily try "How can I use ChatGPT to identify trending topics within my niche and create relevant content that resonates with my target audience?" or "What are some examples of trending topics within my niche that ChatGPT can help me generate blog posts about to ensure my content remains engaging and shareable?"

Furthermore, ChatGPT can generate many engaging blogs post ideas based on your blog's niche and target audience. By leveraging AI's capabilities, you can consistently produce diverse content that caters to your readers' interests and keeps them coming back for more.

Producing well-researched, high-quality content is crucial for attracting and retaining readers. ChatGPT can help you create in-depth, informative articles that showcase your expertise and establish your blog as your niche's go-to source of information. By publishing valuable content, you'll attract more visitors and improve your search engine rankings, further driving organic traffic to your site.

Just ask, "How can ChatGPT help me create well-researched, in-depth articles that showcase my expertise and establish my blog as a go-to source of information within my niche?" or "What are some techniques or tips that ChatGPT can offer to ensure my content is of the highest quality and appeals to my target audience?"

Regarding promoting your content, ChatGPT can assist you in crafting compelling social media posts, email newsletters, and other promotional materials that entice readers to visit your blog. This comprehensive approach to content marketing will help you expand your reach and attract a loyal audience.

As a millionaire in the making, remember that growing your blog's traffic and audience takes time, effort, and consistency. By leveraging ChatGPT's capabilities and maintaining a data-driven content marketing strategy, you'll be well on your way to building a thriving, profitable blog that generates a substantial income and ultimately helps you achieve financially free status.

Utilizing social media, Email Marketing, and Guest Posting

It's important to leverage all available channels to promote your blog and engage with your audience. Social media, email marketing, and guest posting are powerful tools to help you achieve your goals. In this guide, we'll discuss how ChatGPT can assist you in making the most of these channels and maximizing your blog's potential. This is just a brief look at social media. You can find out more in Chapter 4: Social Media Management and Growth.

Social media is an indispensable platform for blog promotion. ChatGPT can help you craft attention-grabbing social media posts that resonate with your target audience and encourage them to visit your blog. By leveraging AI's ability to generate engaging content, you can maintain a consistent and appealing online presence across various platforms such as Facebook, Twitter, Instagram, and LinkedIn. A strong social media presence will drive traffic to your blog and help you build brand awareness and establish relationships with your audience.

Just ask, "How can I use ChatGPT to create engaging social media posts that resonate with my target audience and effectively promote my blog across various platforms?" or "What are some examples of attention-grabbing social media posts generated by ChatGPT that can help me maintain a consistent and appealing online presence?"

Email marketing is another effective way to grow your blog's traffic and audience. ChatGPT can assist you in designing compelling email newsletters that keep your subscribers informed about your latest content and any promotions you're running. With personalized and engaging email content, you'll foster loyalty among your audience and encourage them to share your blog with others, expanding your reach.

Just ask ChatGPT, "How can ChatGPT assist me in crafting personalized and engaging email newsletters to keep my subscribers informed and encourage them to share my blog with others?" or "What are some tips or best practices for using ChatGPT to design email newsletters that foster loyalty among my audience and expand my reach?"

Guest posting is an excellent strategy to gain exposure in your niche and attract new readers to your blog. ChatGPT can help you create high-quality guest posts that showcase your expertise and provide value to the readers of other blogs in your niche. By contributing insightful content to reputable sites, you'll gain valuable backlinks to boost your search engine rankings and increase your credibility and authority in your niche.

By utilizing ChatGPT's AI capabilities to streamline content creation for social media, email marketing, and guest posting, you'll save time and effort while maintaining a consistent and engaging online presence. This consistent, high-quality content will help drive more traffic to your blog, grow your email list, and increase your overall reach and influence. As a result, you'll be well on your way to achieving the financial success and recognition that comes with being a successful and financially free blogger.

Measuring Your Blog's Performance

Maximizing your blog's growth and revenue potential is key to becoming a successful millionaire blogger. One crucial aspect of this process is regularly tracking and analyzing your blog's performance. In this guide, we'll discuss how ChatGPT can support your data analysis efforts and help you make informed decisions that boost your blog's profitability and audience growth.

By monitoring key performance indicators (KPIs) such as traffic, engagement, conversions, and revenue, you can identify areas for improvement and optimize your content and marketing strategies. To assist you in this process, ChatGPT can generate comprehensive reports that provide a detailed overview of your blog's performance. These reports can optimize information on user demographics, top-performing content, sources of traffic, and more. With this data, you can make data-driven decisions to enhance your blog's performance.

Just ask, "How can I use ChatGPT to generate detailed reports on my blog's performance, including user demographics, top-performing content, and sources of traffic?" or "What are some examples of key performance indicators (KPIs) that ChatGPT can help me track and analyze to optimize my content and marketing strategies?"

ChatGPT's AI-driven insights can also help you interpret complex data sets and identify patterns that might go unnoticed. For instance, AI can analyze the relationship between the time of day you publish your content and the resulting engagement levels. You can fine-tune your publishing schedule by identifying these correlations to maximize audience engagement.

It's simple to get a quality answer if you ask, "How can ChatGPT assist me in interpreting complex data sets and uncovering patterns that might go unnoticed, such as the relationship between publishing time and audience engagement?" or "What are some other examples of patterns or correlations that ChatGPT can help me identify to optimize my blog's performance and audience engagement?"

Moreover, ChatGPT can provide actionable insights and recommendations to improve your blog's performance. Based on the data analysis, the AI might suggest optimizing specific blog posts for search engines, promoting underperforming content on social media, or even adjusting your monetization strategies. These insights allow you to implement effective strategies that drive results and boost your blog's profitability.

By leveraging ChatGPT's AI-driven insights, you'll be better equipped to make informed decisions and adapt your content and marketing strategies to maximize your blog's growth and revenue potential. As a result, you'll be well on your way to achieving the financial success and recognition that comes with being an above average blogger. Remember, the key to growing your blog's traffic and audience like a millionaire is staying informed, adapting your strategies based on data, and continuously optimizing your blog's performance.

Streamlining Your Blogging Workflow

Using ChatGPT for Proofreading

A well-written, engaging, and error-free blog is the foundation of a successful and profitable blogging venture. You must understand the importance of maintaining high standards for your blog's content. This is where ChatGPT can serve as an invaluable tool in streamlining your blogging workflow, particularly in the proofreading process.

Proofreading is critical in content creation, ensuring your writing is free of spelling, grammar, and punctuation mistakes. ChatGPT's advanced language understanding capabilities make it an ideal proofreading assistant, helping you identify and correct errors while providing suggestions for improving sentence structure, clarity, and overall flow. You can refine your content by leveraging ChatGPT's AI-driven insights, enhancing its quality and readability.

Just ask ChatGPT, "What are some examples of sentence structure or clarity improvements that ChatGPT can suggest during proofreading?"

Using ChatGPT for proofreading helps maintain a high standard of writing but also positions you as an authority in your niche. This credibility can lead to more revenue-generating opportunities, as readers are more likely to trust and engage with your content. Moreover, high-quality content is more likely to be shared and linked to, increasing your blog's reach and visibility.

In addition to proofreading, ChatGPT can support you in other aspects of your blogging workflow, such as brainstorming topics, conducting research, and even drafting entire blog posts. By harnessing the power of ChatGPT, you can save time and effort, allowing you to focus on other critical aspects of your blog's growth, such as marketing and monetization strategies.

Using ChatGPT to streamline your blogging workflow is a smart investment in your blog's long-term success. By consistently delivering high-quality, error-free content, you'll attract and retain a loyal audience, generate more revenue, and establish your blog as your niche's go-to source of information. Remember, the key to achieving millionaire status in the blogging world is to work smarter, not harder, and ChatGPT can be an essential tool in your journey towards success.

Leveraging ChatGPT to Generate Content Ideas

You need to understand the importance of consistently generating fresh, engaging, and relevant content ideas to fuel your blog's success. This is where ChatGPT's AI-driven brainstorming capabilities can be a game-changer, helping you stay ahead of industry trends and keep your content calendar full.

By leveraging ChatGPT's advanced language model, you can generate many topic ideas and outlines tailored to your niche and target audience's interests. This AI-driven approach ensures that your blog remains a valuable resource for your readers, attracting more visitors and boosting your search engine rankings. Higher rankings and increased visibility create new monetization possibilities, allowing you to capitalize on the valuable content you're producing.

For instance, ChatGPT can analyze your niche and target audience to identify gaps in the market or emerging trends that you can explore in your blog posts. By staying ahead of the curve and addressing these topics, you position yourself as a thought leader in your niche, creating trust and credibility with your audience. This credibility can translate into increased engagement, more backlinks, and higher conversion rates for your monetization strategies, such as affiliate marketing or sponsored content.

Get a great answer by asking, "How can I use ChatGPT to identify gaps in the market and emerging trends within my niche and target audience of millennials?" or "What steps should I follow to leverage ChatGPT in uncovering content opportunities that can position me as a thought leader?"

Beyond generating content ideas, ChatGPT can also help you create a comprehensive content plan by identifying your blog posts' best formats, target keywords, and distribution channels. By incorporating this strategic planning into your blogging workflow, you can work more efficiently and produce content that resonates with your audience and drives results.

Leveraging ChatGPT for content idea generation is an investment in your blog's long-term success. By consistently delivering high-quality, engaging, and relevant content, you'll create a loyal audience, generate more revenue, and establish your blog as your niche's go-to source of information. Remember, the key to achieving millionaire status in the blogging world is to work smarter, not harder, and ChatGPT can be an essential ally in your journey towards success.

Saving Time and Increasing Productivity

As an already successful blogger would recognize too that time is one of your most valuable assets. In the blogging world, efficiency is critical for maximizing revenue potential, and ChatGPT can play a significant role in streamlining your blogging workflow.

You can save substantial time and effort by utilizing ChatGPT for various aspects of your blogging business, such as content ideation, writing, proofreading, social media management, and email marketing. This time-saving advantage allows you to focus on other crucial aspects of your blogging business, such as networking, strategic planning, or expanding your product and service offerings.

You can ask, "What steps should I follow to use ChatGPT in crafting engaging social media posts and email newsletters?" or "How can ChatGPT help me maintain a consistent online presence while freeing time for audience engagement?"

For example, ChatGPT's advanced language model can help you craft engaging social media posts and email newsletters in a fraction of the time it would take you to create them manually. This efficiency not only allows you to maintain a consistent online presence but also frees up time for you to engage with your audience, respond to comments, and establish meaningful connections that can lead to new opportunities and collaborations.

Another area where ChatGPT can boost your productivity is by automating the research process for your blog posts. The AI can quickly gather relevant information, statistics, and resources, allowing you to focus on creating high-quality content that resonates with your audience. This streamlined approach ensures that you can maintain a consistent publishing schedule, essential for retaining and growing your readership.

Ask, "How can I leverage ChatGPT to gather relevant information, statistics, and resources quickly and efficiently for my blog posts?" or "What are some best practices for using ChatGPT to streamline my research process, ensuring the quality of my content?"

Millionaires in the making are already leveraging ChatGPT to streamline their blogging workflow as a strategic investment in their blog's long-term success. By working more efficiently, you can achieve a higher level of productivity, maintain a consistent publishing schedule, and ultimately generate more income from your blog too.

Remember, the key to achieving millionaire status in blogging is to work smarter, not harder. ChatGPT can be your secret weapon in your journey towards success, providing AI-driven support that allows you to focus on what truly matters: creating valuable content, connecting with your audience, and building a profitable blogging empire.

Chapter 4: Social Media Management and Growth

The Power of social media in Business

The Importance of a strong social media presence

This has become a crucial component of any successful business strategy in today's digital age. Making it in the digital marketing age is easier than ever. You understand that effectively leveraging social media's power can significantly enhance brand awareness, engage with your target audience, and drive revenue growth. ChatGPT, with its advanced AI capabilities, can play a pivotal role in helping you achieve these objectives.

Using ChatGPT to create captivating content tailored to your followers, you can attract attention and spark engagement on your social media channels. High-quality content is vital for fostering connections with your audience and increasing the likelihood of conversions, leading to more income-generation opportunities.

For example, ChatGPT can generate content ideas, craft compelling captions, and suggest eye-catching visuals that resonate with your followers. This level of customization ensures that your social media content aligns with your brand identity and caters to the unique interests of your audience. As a result, your social media channels become an indispensable tool for building relationships with potential customers, nurturing leads, and ultimately driving sales.

By leveraging ChatGPT to analyze your audience's demographics, preferences, and online behaviors, you can refine your content strategy to target the right users at the right time, increasing your chances of achieving a high return on investment.

Just ask, "How can I leverage ChatGPT to analyze my audience's demographics, preferences, and online behaviors for a more effective social media strategy?" or "What is the latest viral content, and key influencers within my niche for collaboration and cross-promotion opportunities?"

ChatGPT can also help you identify trends, viral content, and key influencers within your niche, allowing you to capitalize on opportunities for collaboration, cross-promotion, and even content co-creation. These partnerships can amplify your brand's reach, opening new markets and revenue streams.

Identifying the right platforms for your target audience

In the world of social media, a one-size-fits-all approach is rarely effective. You understand the importance of identifying the right platforms for your target audience to maximize your online presence and income-generating potential. With the assistance of ChatGPT, you can analyze user data and identify trends, ensuring that your social media efforts are targeted and effective.

To begin, ChatGPT can help you conduct research and gather valuable insights into the demographics and preferences of your target audience. This information will enable you to understand which social media platforms are best suited for reaching your desired customer base. Focusing on the most relevant platforms allows you to allocate your resources more efficiently and boost your social media investment return.

Just ask, "How can I use ChatGPT to research and gather insights into my target audience's demographics and preferences to identify the most relevant social media platforms?" or "What steps should I take to leverage ChatGPT to monitor emerging social media platforms and evaluate their potential for my business?"

Once you have identified the right platforms, ChatGPT can assist you in crafting platform-specific content that caters to each channel's unique features and user behaviors. For example, Instagram might be ideal for showcasing visually appealing images and short videos, while LinkedIn is more suitable for sharing professional insights and industry news. By tailoring your content to the platform, you increase the likelihood of engaging your target audience and converting them into customers.

ChatGPT can also help you stay ahead of the curve by monitoring emerging social media platforms and analyzing their potential for your business. Early adoption of new platforms can give you a competitive advantage and provide additional income-generating opportunities by tapping into new markets and audiences.

Recognizing that a successful social media strategy requires constant adaptation and fine-tuning is essential. By leveraging ChatGPT's AI-driven capabilities, you can analyze the performance of your social media efforts across different platforms and adjust your approach accordingly. This data-driven decision-making process will ensure that your social media presence remains relevant, engaging, and effective at driving revenue growth.

Setting clear goals and objectives for your social media strategy

As a future social media business owner, you understand the importance of setting clear goals and objectives for your social media strategy. You can measure your progress by establishing specific targets, optimizing your approach, and ultimately driving better results. ChatGPT can play a pivotal role in defining and refining your goals and tracking your performance against these objectives.

Initially, ChatGPT can help you outline your social media goals, considering your unique business objectives and target audience. These goals could include increasing brand awareness, driving website traffic, generating leads, or fostering community engagement. Clearly defining your goals establishes a solid foundation for your social media strategy and sets the stage for success.

You can easily ask, "How can I use ChatGPT to help me outline my social media goals and objectives based on my unique business and target audience?" or "What steps should I take with ChatGPT to break down my goals into actionable steps and set up a social media content calendar?"

Once your goals are established, ChatGPT can assist you in breaking them down into actionable steps and setting up a social media content calendar. By leveraging ChatGPT's AI capabilities, you can plan your content and promotional efforts, ensuring that your approach aligns with your objectives and contributes to income-generating activities.

ChatGPT can also be invaluable in helping you stay on track and measure your progress against your goals. By providing regular performance reports and insights, ChatGPT enables you to identify areas for improvement and make data-driven decisions that enhance your social media strategy. This ongoing analysis and optimization will ensure your social media efforts remain focused and effective.

You can ask ChatGPT, "How can I leverage ChatGPT to monitor my progress against my social media goals and provide performance reports and insights?" or "What strategies can I use with ChatGPT to identify new income-generating opportunities on social media and optimize my approach for maximum results?"

In addition to tracking your performance, ChatGPT can help you identify new income-generating opportunities on social media. For example, it can analyze your audience's interests and preferences, allowing you to create targeted sponsored content, identify potential collaboration partners, or discover new advertising possibilities. By staying attuned to these opportunities, you can maximize your revenue potential and strengthen your position as a leader in your niche.

By using ChatGPT to streamline your social media management, you can focus on the tasks that directly contribute to your income, such as securing sponsored posts, fostering collaborations, or growing your audience to increase advertising revenue. This efficient approach will enable you to make the most of your social media presence, capitalizing on every opportunity to generate income and build a lasting, profitable business.

In summary, setting clear goals and objectives for your social media strategy is critical to ensuring long-term success and growth. With ChatGPT's assistance, you can define, track, and optimize your goals, unlocking the full potential of your social media presence and maximizing your income-generating opportunities. By embracing AI technology and harnessing the power of social media, you can pave the way for a prosperous and thriving entrepreneurial journey.

Content Creation with ChatGPT

Crafting engaging and shareable social media posts

Picture this: you're on your way to becoming a millionaire, and you know that creating engaging and shareable social media content is essential for your success. The good news is that ChatGPT can be your secret weapon, enabling you to produce high-quality content that drives engagement consistently, increases your reach, and ultimately boosts your income potential through sponsored posts and collaborations.

Imagine the excitement of watching your follower count grow as your captivating content spreads across social media platforms, attracting attention and sparking conversations. By leveraging the power of AI, you'll be able to craft posts that resonate with your audience, leading to more likes, shares, and comments that can translate into increased revenue opportunities.

ChatGPT's advanced language capabilities allow you to create content tailored to your audience's interests and preferences, ensuring that your posts strike a chord with your followers. Whether you need attention-grabbing headlines, thought-provoking questions, or share-worthy snippets of information, ChatGPT has you covered.

You can ask, "Write me an article that includes French quotes and references from live websites about my [your niche] niche" or "Generate engaging social media headlines that incorporate popular idioms or expressions from various languages related to my [your niche] niche, to captivate a diverse audience."

Moreover, ChatGPT can help you generate content ideas and maintain a consistent posting schedule, ensuring you always have fresh, engaging material to share with your audience. This consistent flow of content will keep your followers engaged while signaling to potential sponsors and collaborators that you're a reliable and valuable partner.

Using ChatGPT to create content that reflects your unique voice and brand, you can establish yourself as an authority in your niche, further increasing your appeal to potential partners. This credibility can open new income-generating opportunities, such as sponsored posts, brand partnerships, and even affiliate marketing deals.

Of course, the world of social media is always evolving, so it's crucial to stay ahead of the curve. ChatGPT can help you identify and capitalize on emerging trends, ensuring your content remains fresh, relevant, and appealing to your audience. By staying attuned to these shifts, you can maintain your competitive edge and grow your income potential.

Just ask, "How can I use ChatGPT to develop a series of social media challenges or contests that encourage user-generated content and engagement in my [your niche] niche?" or "What are some innovative ways to repurpose existing content using ChatGPT, allowing me to maintain a fresh and diverse social media presence in my [your niche] niche?"

So, for all aspiring millionaires, remember that crafting engaging, and shareable social media posts is critical to your journey to success. By harnessing the power of ChatGPT, you can consistently produce top-notch content that captivates your audience, expands your reach, and paves the way for lucrative income-generating opportunities. Embrace the potential of AI-driven content creation and watch as your social media presence flourishes, propelling you towards your goal of financial success.

Utilizing ChatGPT for hashtag research and trend analysis

You might not be yet, but soon you will be a millionaire, and you must stay eager to unlock the full potential of your social media presence. You know that staying on top of current trends and using relevant hashtags is vital for increasing your visibility and attracting lucrative opportunities. Excitingly, ChatGPT is here to help you achieve this goal with its powerful AI capabilities, which can assist you in conducting hashtag research and analyzing trends.

Harness the power of ChatGPT to identify popular and relevant hashtags that resonate with your target audience. By strategically incorporating these hashtags into your content, you'll be able to reach more users, engage with potential followers, and increase your overall visibility on social media platforms. This heightened visibility can lead to more opportunities for monetization, such as sponsored content, influencer partnerships, and affiliate marketing deals.

In addition to hashtag research, ChatGPT can help you stay ahead of the curve by analyzing current trends and identifying emerging topics that your audience will find engaging. By creating content that reflects these trends, you'll be able to demonstrate your expertise, connect with your followers, and, ultimately, unlock new income-generating opportunities.

You can easily ask, "What are the top 10 trending hashtags in my [your niche] niche for this week, and how can I create content around them to boost my social media engagement?" or "What are some emerging trends in my [your niche] niche that I should be aware of, and how can I incorporate them into my content strategy to stay ahead of the competition?"

Picture the excitement of watching your social media engagement soar as you incorporate the latest trends and hashtags into your content. You'll see your follower count grow, attracting the attention of potential sponsors and partners eager to work with a social media-savvy influencer like you. With ChatGPT's support, you can seize these opportunities with confidence, knowing that your content is always fresh, relevant, and aligned with what your audience wants to see.

But that's not all. ChatGPT can also help you plan your content calendar, ensuring that you maintain a consistent posting schedule and never miss an opportunity to capitalize on a hot trend or hashtag. By keeping your content current and engaging, you'll be able to foster a loyal community of followers who eagerly anticipate your posts, further increasing your appeal to potential partners and sponsors.

So, for all the future millionaires out there, remember that using ChatGPT for hashtag research and trend analysis can be a game-changer in your quest for social media success. By strategically incorporating popular hashtags and trends into your content, you'll be able to attract more followers, boost engagement, and ultimately, unlock the income-generating opportunities you've been dreaming of. Embrace the potential of AI-driven content creation and watch as your social media presence skyrockets, propelling you towards your goal of financial freedom.

Creating captivating visuals and captions with ChatGPT's assistance

As an aspiring millionaire, eager to harness the power of social media to boost your income potential. You know captivating visuals and captions are essential for grabbing your audience's attention and driving engagement. ChatGPT is excited to help you achieve this goal with its creative capabilities, enabling you to craft engaging captions and descriptions that complement your visuals.

In the fast-paced world of social media, standing out from the competition is vital for success. By utilizing ChatGPT's creativity, you'll be able to craft unique captions that capture your audience's attention and encourage them to engage with your content. This heightened engagement can increase visibility and a growing follower base, making you more attractive to potential sponsors and partners eager to work with an influential social media personality.

Furthermore, ChatGPT can also help you brainstorm ideas for eye-catching visuals that resonate with your target audience. By combining your creativity with the power of AI, you can produce stunning images and graphics that captivate your followers and drive higher engagement rates. This visual appeal will boost your social media presence and increase the likelihood of monetization through sponsored posts, brand collaborations, and advertising revenue.

To help with your decision-making, ask, "Can you help me create an engaging caption for this [describe your visual] that will capture my audience's attention and encourage them to interact with my content?" or "What are some creative concepts for visuals that will resonate with my target audience in the [your niche] niche and make my social media posts stand out?"

Imagine the excitement of watching your social media engagement skyrocket as you post captivating visuals paired with attention-grabbing captions. You'll see your follower count grow and attract the attention of potential sponsors and partners who recognize the value of working with a visually engaging and creative social media influencer. With ChatGPT's support, you'll be able to seize these opportunities with confidence, knowing that your content is always fresh, visually appealing, and enticing to your audience.

In addition to helping, you create engaging visuals and captions, ChatGPT can support your social media growth strategy in other ways, such as by identifying the best times to post your content, monitoring your performance, and suggesting optimizations to enhance your results. By leveraging the power of AI, you'll be able to maximize your social media presence, unlocking new income-generating opportunities that bring you closer to your goal of financial success.

To help with this, ask, "How can I optimize my social media posting schedule to maximize engagement and reach for my [your niche] content?" or "Based on my current social media performance, what recommendations do you have for improving my visual content and captions to boost engagement and attract more followers in the [your niche] niche?"

So, if you want to be part of the future millionaire's club, remember that using ChatGPT to create captivating visuals and captions can be a game-changer in your quest for social media success. By strategically combining eye-catching images with compelling captions, you'll be able to attract more followers, boost engagement, and ultimately unlock the income-generating opportunities you've been dreaming of. Embrace the potential of AI-driven content creation and watch as your social media presence blossoms, propelling you towards becoming a millionaire.

Building and Engaging Your Community

Growing your followers and expanding your reach

Imagine the thrill of watching your social media following grow exponentially, with more and more people engaging with your content daily. As an aspiring millionaire, you understand that building a large, loyal community is essential for generating income through social media. Excitingly, ChatGPT can be your secret weapon in achieving this goal, helping you create posts that resonate with your target audience and attract new followers.

One of the keys to social media success is staying ahead of trends and producing content that appeals to your community. By leveraging ChatGPT's AI capabilities, you can identify trending topics, analyze your followers' preferences, and craft tailor-made content that keeps your audience engaged and eager for more. As your reach expands, so do your monetization opportunities. ChatGPT becomes an invaluable tool in your social media growth efforts, ensuring you stay one step ahead of the competition.

But the power of ChatGPT goes beyond content creation. By assisting you in analyzing your audience's behavior, preferences, and demographics, ChatGPT can help you develop a more targeted and effective engagement strategy. This means you can build deeper connections with your followers, transforming them into a loyal community that advocates for your brand and amplifies your message. This loyal community is what brands and partners seek when they invest in influencer partnerships and sponsored content, creating lucrative income opportunities for you.

You can ask, "Can you provide me with a list of trending topics in my [your niche] niche that I can create engaging content around to attract new followers and expand my reach?" or "How can I analyze my current audience's preferences and demographics to tailor my content more effectively and drive increased engagement?"

Interaction is another vital aspect of building and engaging your community. With ChatGPT's help, you can craft personalized responses to comments and messages, ensuring your audience feels heard and valued. By consistently interacting with your followers, you'll be able to foster a sense of belonging within your community, leading to higher engagement rates and increased opportunities for monetization.

Now, picture the excitement of seeing your follower count soar, and your community becomes more engaged. As your social media presence gains momentum, you'll attract the attention of potential sponsors and partners who recognize the value of working with an influential content creator. With ChatGPT's support, you can confidently seize these opportunities, knowing you have the tools and resources needed to maintain a thriving, engaged community.

You can ask ChatGPT, "What are some tips for crafting personalized responses to comments and messages that will make my followers feel valued and heard in my [your niche] community?" or "How can I adjust my engagement strategy to foster a sense of belonging within my community and boost interaction, ultimately leading to more opportunities for monetization?"

In conclusion, embracing the potential of ChatGPT to build and engage your community can be a game-changer in your social media growth journey. By leveraging AI-driven content creation, audience analysis, and personalized interactions, you'll be able to attract more followers, boost engagement, and unlock the income-generating opportunities you've been dreaming of. Embrace the power of AI and watch as your social media presence blossoms, propelling you towards your goal of becoming a millionaire.

Interacting with your audience and fostering engagement

Imagine yourself, as a future millionaire with a thriving social media presence and a passionate, engaged community of followers. To achieve this vision, you understand that interacting with your audience is essential for building trust and fostering long-term relationships. However, staying connected with your community can become increasingly time-consuming as your following grows. Thankfully, ChatGPT can help streamline this process, enabling you to focus on other aspects of your social media empire while maintaining a strong connection with your audience.

Imagine the excitement of watching your audience engagement skyrocket as you leverage ChatGPT's AI capabilities to craft personalized responses to comments, questions, and direct messages. Using AI to manage your interactions efficiently allows you to maintain an active and engaged community without sacrificing your valuable time. This high level of engagement creates a solid foundation for your income-generating activities. An engaged audience is likelier to participate in collaborations, sponsored content, and other opportunities that contribute to your financial success.

You can try asking ChatGPT, "How can I use ChatGPT to efficiently craft personalized responses to comments, questions, and direct messages while maintaining authenticity and building trust within my community?" or "What are some strategies for staying connected with my growing audience without sacrificing too much of my valuable time?"

With ChatGPT's assistance, you can stay on top of trending topics and community discussions, ensuring your responses and interactions remain relevant and timely. By demonstrating your understanding of your audience's interests and concerns, you can build trust and authenticity that makes your community even more loyal and engaged. This loyalty translates into increased opportunities for monetization, as brands and partners value influencers who can maintain a genuine connection with their followers. Moreover, as your follower count grows and your reach expands, you'll find yourself with an ever-increasing number of collaboration and sponsorship opportunities. ChatGPT can help you manage these exciting prospects by assisting in crafting proposals, pitches, and negotiation tactics. As you leverage the power of AI to secure lucrative deals and collaborations, you'll be one step closer to achieving your entrepreneurial dreams.

Just ask, "How can ChatGPT help me stay on top of trending topics and community discussions to ensure my responses and interactions remain relevant and timely?" or "In what ways can I use ChatGPT to assist in crafting proposals, pitches, and negotiation tactics for securing lucrative collaborations and sponsorships that will contribute to my financial success?"

In conclusion, embracing ChatGPT to interact with your audience and foster engagement can be a game-changer in your journey towards becoming a millionaire, and giving you the type of hope to keep pressing on in your journey. By utilizing AI-driven personalized responses and staying relevant in your community, you can build trust and loyalty among your followers. This, in turn, will lead to increased opportunities for monetization through collaborations, sponsored content, and other income-generating activities. So, harness the power of AI to transform your social media presence and propel yourself towards a future filled with success and financial abundance.

Using ChatGPT to streamline community management tasks

Effective community management is vital for maintaining a strong and active social media presence, which is key to unlocking monetization opportunities. ChatGPT can help you stay on top of your community management tasks, such as moderating comments, scheduling posts, and analyzing your audience's preferences.

You can quickly ask, "How can I utilize ChatGPT to effectively moderate comments and maintain a positive, engaging atmosphere within my social media community?" or "What are some strategies to use ChatGPT for scheduling posts that align with my audience's preferences and maximize engagement?"

With ChatGPT's assistance, you can ensure your social media profiles remain organized and well-maintained, allowing you to focus on creating high-quality content and exploring new avenues for income generation. By streamlining your community management, ChatGPT can help you unlock the full potential of your social media presence and maximize your earning opportunities.

Just ask, "In what ways can I leverage ChatGPT to analyze my audience's preferences and tailor my content strategy to better appeal to their interests?" or "What is the best programming language to use to build a Facebook API social media management app?"

Social Media Advertising and Promotion

Implementing effective ad campaigns on various platforms

Successfully harnessing the power of social media advertising to generate income and expand your reach. To achieve this vision, you understand that it's crucial to identify the platforms best suited for your target audience and craft ads that resonate with them. ChatGPT can be the secret weapon in your arsenal, helping you develop impactful ad campaigns that drive traffic, increase conversions, and maximize your return on investment.

Picture the excitement of watching your ad campaigns flourish as you leverage ChatGPT's AI capabilities to analyze your target audience's preferences and generate tailored content for each platform. By creating targeted ads that appeal to potential customers, you can effectively expand your reach, attract new followers, and unlock a myriad of income-generating opportunities.

With ChatGPT's assistance, you can stay ahead of the curve by identifying emerging trends and capitalizing on them through your advertising efforts. The AI-powered tool can help you develop and test various ad concepts, allowing you to optimize your campaigns for maximum engagement and conversion. As your ads gain traction, you'll be able to attract new customers, secure lucrative partnerships, and elevate your brand's reputation.

Just ask ChatGPT prompt, "How can I use ChatGPT to identify the most suitable social media platforms for my target audience and create ads that resonate with them?" or "What are the steps to leverage ChatGPT's AI capabilities for developing impactful ad campaigns that drive traffic and increase conversions?"

Moreover, ChatGPT can help you make data-driven decisions about your ad campaigns, from determining the optimal budget allocation across platforms to identifying the most effective ad formats for your specific audience. By leveraging AI-driven insights, you can fine-tune your advertising strategy to achieve the best possible results, ensuring that every dollar you invest in your campaigns contributes to your goal of becoming a millionaire.

As you continue to refine your ad campaigns with the help of ChatGPT, you'll also be able to explore new and innovative ways to promote your brand and offerings. This might include experimenting with influencer marketing, sponsored content, or even creating your viral challenges that drive massive engagement and brand awareness. With ChatGPT by your side, the possibilities are virtually limitless, and the sky's the limit for your social media advertising success.

You can ask, "How can ChatGPT help me make data-driven decisions for optimizing my advertising strategy, such as budget allocation and choosing effective ad formats?" or "What are some innovative ways to promote my brand and offerings using ChatGPT, such as influencer marketing, sponsored content, or viral challenges?"

In conclusion, utilizing ChatGPT to implement effective ad campaigns on various platforms can be a game-changer in your journey towards becoming a powerful social media profile. By leveraging AI-powered insights and creating targeted ads that resonate with your audience, you can drive traffic, increase conversions, and maximize your return on investment. Embrace the power of AI to transform your social media advertising efforts and propel yourself towards a future filled with success and financial abundance.

Crafting persuasive ad copy with ChatGPT's support

You thought you couldn't be a millionaire, well now by leveraging the power of social media advertising to generate substantial income and grow your business it's possible. To turn this dream into reality, you know that crafting persuasive and engaging ad copy is essential. This is where ChatGPT comes into play, providing invaluable support in creating compelling ad copy that grabs your audience's attention and encourages them to act.

Feel the excitement as you utilize ChatGPT's AI capabilities to generate captivating ideas and refine your messaging. ChatGPT's assistance ensures that your ad copy is tailor-made for your target audience, striking a chord with their preferences, interests, and pain points. As a result, your ads will stand out from the competition and drive significant results, ultimately leading to increased income and business growth. Imagine the satisfaction of watching your social media advertising campaigns flourish, as ChatGPT helps you create a variety of ad copy styles that resonate with different segments of your audience. This versatility allows you to cater to diverse preferences and effectively communicate the value of your offerings. By crafting an ad copy that speaks directly to your target market, you'll be able to generate higher click-through rates, improved conversion rates, and ultimately, increased revenue.

You can ask, "How can ChatGPT help me create compelling ad copy that captures my audience's attention and encourages them to take action?" or "What techniques can I use with ChatGPT to generate captivating ideas and refine my messaging for my target audience?"

With ChatGPT by your side, you can fearlessly experiment with your ad copy, testing various headlines, calls to action, and emotional triggers to identify the most effective combinations. As you optimize your ad copy, you'll discover new ways to connect with your audience and inspire them to engage with your brand. This continuous improvement will further elevate your social media advertising efforts, propelling you closer to your goal of becoming a millionaire. Additionally, ChatGPT can help you stay up to date with the latest trends and best practices in social media advertising, ensuring your ad copy remains fresh, relevant, and impactful. By staying ahead of the curve and adapting your messaging to the ever-changing landscape, you'll be able to captivate your audience and maintain a competitive edge in the crowded digital space.

Try asking, "How can I use ChatGPT to experiment with different ad copy elements like headlines, calls to action, and emotional triggers to optimize my campaigns?" or "What are the latest trends and best practices in social media advertising that ChatGPT can help me incorporate into my ad copy to stay fresh and relevant?"

In summary, embracing ChatGPT's support in crafting persuasive ad copy can be a game-changer in your pursuit of becoming a millionaire. By leveraging AI-powered insights and creating engaging, tailor-made content that resonates with your target audience, you can drive impressive results and accelerate your business growth. Seize the opportunity to harness the power of AI and let ChatGPT guide you on your exciting journey towards financial success and abundance.

Analyzing and optimizing your ad performance

Leveraging the power of social media advertising to skyrocket your income and build your business empire. The key to unlocking your full income potential lies in analyzing and optimizing your ad performance, and ChatGPT can help you easily achieve this.

Feel the thrill as you monitor your social media advertising campaigns, using ChatGPT's advanced AI capabilities to uncover valuable insights and pinpoint areas for improvement. By identifying trends and untapped opportunities, you can make data-driven decisions that will elevate your ad campaigns and bring you closer to your millionaire goals. Embrace the excitement of continuous improvement, as ChatGPT assists you in refining your advertising efforts. With its support, you can iterate and experiment with different ad formats, targeting options, and messaging styles to uncover the winning combination that resonates with your audience. As you optimize your campaigns, you'll see your engagement rates soar, conversions increase, and ultimately, your income grows exponentially.

To aid with this, ask, "How can ChatGPT help me analyze my social media ad performance and uncover valuable insights to improve my campaigns?" or "What are the key metrics I should focus on when using ChatGPT to evaluate the effectiveness of my social media advertising efforts?"

Let ChatGPT be your trusted partner in your pursuit of financial success, providing you with up-to-date information on the latest industry trends and best practices. By staying informed and adapting your advertising strategy to the ever-changing social media landscape, you'll maintain a competitive edge and ensure your ad campaigns continue to drive impressive results.

As you watch your ad performance improve, you'll experience a sense of accomplishment and satisfaction, knowing that you're making the most of your social media advertising budget. With ChatGPT's guidance, you can maximize your return on investment and transform your social media presence into a powerful income-generating machine.

Just ask, "How can I use ChatGPT to iterate and experiment with different ad formats, targeting options, and messaging styles to optimize my ad campaigns?" or "What are the latest industry trends and best practices that ChatGPT can help me stay informed about to maintain a competitive edge in my social media advertising strategy?"

In conclusion, using ChatGPT to analyze and optimize your social media ad performance can play a pivotal role in your journey towards becoming a millionaire. By tapping into AI-powered insights and making data-driven decisions, you can fine-tune your advertising efforts and unlock your full income potential. Embrace the excitement of this rewarding process and let ChatGPT propel you towards financial success and abundance.

Monetizing Your Social Media Presence

Exploring revenue streams through sponsored posts

Imagine living the dream of financial abundance by harnessing the power of sponsored posts on social media. With ChatGPT by your side, you can unlock the potential of brand collaborations and turn your social media presence into a goldmine, propelling you towards millionaire status.

Feel the exhilaration of discovering new revenue streams as ChatGPT assists you in identifying lucrative brand partnerships that perfectly align with your niche and audience. By leveraging the AI's capabilities, you can find the ideal brands to collaborate with and create sponsored posts that captivate your followers and generate significant income.

Just ask, "How can ChatGPT help me identify potential brand partnerships that align with my niche and audience?" or "What are some strategies ChatGPT can suggest for approaching brands and securing sponsored post opportunities?"

Experience the thrill of crafting engaging sponsored content with ChatGPT's help. By producing captivating posts that showcase the value of the promoted products, you'll maintain the authenticity of your content while driving results for your brand partners. This powerful combination will not only boost your income but also solidify your reputation as a sought-after influencer in your niche.

Visualize the excitement of watching your income grow as you build strong relationships with brands and establish yourself as an influential figure in your industry. With ChatGPT's support, you can strike the perfect balance between creating authentic, relatable content and promoting products that resonate with your followers. As your sponsored post collaborations flourish, you'll be well on your way to becoming a millionaire.

Just try asking ChatGPT, "How can ChatGPT assist me in creating engaging and authentic sponsored content that resonates with my followers?" or "What are some tips ChatGPT can provide for maintaining strong relationships with brands and optimizing my sponsored post collaborations for maximum income?"

By staying informed about the latest trends and leveraging ChatGPT's powerful AI capabilities, you can make the most of your social media presence and maximize your earnings through sponsored posts. Embrace this thrilling journey towards financial success and let ChatGPT guide you every step of the way, turning your dreams of millionaire status into a reality.

Leveraging ChatGPT to create compelling pitches

In the world of social media, the art of pitching is critical to your success and unlocking your potential as a millionaire. With ChatGPT's support, you can create powerful pitches that open doors to lucrative partnerships, setting you on the path to financial freedom.

ChatGPT's AI capabilities enable you to generate innovative ideas for unique collaborations, ensuring your pitches stand out from the competition. By leveraging this cutting-edge technology, you'll be able to pinpoint the most effective ways to showcase your value to potential brand partners and attract their attention.

Master the art of persuasive messaging with the help of ChatGPT. By crafting convincing pitches that highlight your strengths, audience reach, and the mutual benefits of collaborating with your brand partners, you'll pique their interest and pave the way for fruitful partnerships.

Just ask, "How can ChatGPT help me generate innovative ideas for unique collaborations that will make my pitches stand out?" or "What are some techniques ChatGPT can suggest for effectively showcasing my value to potential brand partners?"

One of the key advantages of using ChatGPT is its ability to create customized pitches tailored to each brand's specific needs and preferences. By producing personalized pitches that resonate with your target brands, you'll increase the likelihood of securing sponsored post opportunities and, in turn, boost your income potential.

Moreover, ChatGPT can help you refine your pitches over time by analyzing the responses and feedback you receive from brands. This invaluable insight allows you to continuously improve your pitching skills and secure even more lucrative collaborations in the future.

You can ask, "How can ChatGPT assist me in crafting persuasive, customized pitches that resonate with my target brands?" or "What are some strategies ChatGPT can provide for refining my pitches over time based on feedback from brands?"

By harnessing the power of ChatGPT, you can become a pitching powerhouse in the world of social media, securing brand partnerships that elevate your income and bring you closer to your goal of one of the most successful profiles in the social media world.

Managing and tracking your social media income

Unlock your potential by effectively managing and tracking your social media income with the support of ChatGPT. By utilizing AI's capabilities, you can stay on top of your earnings and ensure your social media monetization strategies are yielding optimal results.

ChatGPT can revolutionize the way you monitor your social media income by generating detailed income reports that provide a comprehensive overview of your financial progress. These reports will break down your earnings by source, giving you valuable insights into which partnerships and monetization strategies are driving the most revenue.

Just ask ChatGPT, "How can ChatGPT help me generate detailed income reports that provide a comprehensive overview of my financial progress?" or "What insights can ChatGPT offer to help me understand which partnerships and monetization strategies are driving the most revenue?"

Moreover, ChatGPT can assist you in tracking payments from your brand partners, ensuring you never miss an incoming payment or invoice. This level of organization not only simplifies your financial management process but also allows you to focus on your content creation and audience engagement.

By analyzing your income data, ChatGPT can provide actionable insights that guide you in optimizing your monetization strategies. This information empowers you to make informed decisions about which partnerships to pursue, which types of sponsored content perform best, and how to refine your approach to maximize your income potential.

Staying organized and informed about your financial progress is critical to scaling your social media income and achieving your millionaire goals. With ChatGPT's support, you can maintain a clear understanding of your earnings, identify opportunities for growth, and make data-driven decisions that propel you toward financial success.

Quickly ask, "How can ChatGPT assist me in tracking payments from brand partners and ensuring I never miss an incoming payment or invoice?" or "What actionable insights can ChatGPT provide to help me optimize my monetization strategies and maximize my income potential?"

In conclusion, ChatGPT can be an invaluable tool in your journey to becoming a social media millionaire. By helping you manage and track your social media income, ChatGPT empowers you to make the most of your monetization efforts, ensuring continued success in the competitive world of social media.

Measuring Your Social Media Success

Monitoring key performance indicators (KPIs)

Unlock your millionaire potential by harnessing the power of ChatGPT to measure your social media success through the monitoring of key performance indicators (KPIs). Staying on top of these crucial metrics, such as engagement, reach, and conversions, ensures you are making the most of your social media presence and optimizing your revenue opportunities.

With ChatGPT's assistance, you can easily analyze your KPI data, allowing you to assess the effectiveness of your content and strategies. This AI-driven analysis is essential to making data-driven decisions that will boost your social media performance and bring you closer to your millionaire goals.

For instance, ChatGPT can help you identify trends in your engagement metrics, such as likes, comments, and shares, providing valuable insights into which types of content resonate best with your audience. By understanding these trends, you can create more of the content your audience loves, increasing engagement and making your profile more attractive to potential brand partners.

You can ask, "How can ChatGPT help me monitor and analyze key performance indicators (KPIs) to ensure I am making the most of my social media presence?" or "What insights can ChatGPT provide about engagement, reach, and conversions to optimize my revenue opportunities?"

In addition, ChatGPT can support you in tracking your reach and impressions, giving you a clear picture of how well your content is spreading across social media platforms. This invaluable information allows you to adjust your posting strategies, hashtags, and other tactics to maximize your visibility and attract a larger, more engaged following.

Lastly, ChatGPT is essential in monitoring your conversion rates, such as the number of clicks on sponsored posts or affiliate links. By understanding which content and promotion strategies drive the most conversions, you can refine your approach and focus on the tactics that yield the highest return on investment.

Try asking, "How can ChatGPT assist me in identifying trends in engagement metrics like likes, comments, and shares to create more engaging content?" or "What support can ChatGPT offer in tracking my reach, impressions, and conversion rates to refine my approach and maximize my return on investment?"

Armed with this actionable intelligence, you can make informed decisions about which areas of your social media presence need improvement and where to allocate your resources for the greatest impact. With the help of ChatGPT, you can stay on top of your social media performance, continually refine your strategies, and drive your income to new heights.

Using ChatGPT for sentiment analysis and insights

Maximizing your social media success and unlocking your millionaire dreams requires a deep understanding of your audience's sentiment towards your content and brand partnerships. ChatGPT is the perfect tool for conducting sentiment analysis on user comments and reactions, providing essential insights into how your followers perceive your content and sponsored collaborations.

By harnessing the power of ChatGPT for sentiment analysis, you can identify the types of content and brand collaborations that resonate with your audience. This critical information allows you to focus on creating content and establishing partnerships that align with your followers' preferences, leading to higher engagement rates and an increased income potential from successful brand collaborations.

Just ask, "How can ChatGPT help me conduct sentiment analysis on user comments and reactions to better understand my audience's perception of my content and brand partnerships?" or "What insights can ChatGPT provide through sentiment analysis to improve my engagement rates and increase my income potential from successful brand collaborations?"

Imagine the possibilities: ChatGPT can process vast amounts of data from user comments and reactions, generating a clear picture of your audience's sentiment. By understanding their likes and dislikes, you can make strategic decisions to improve your content and choose brand partners that genuinely appeal to your followers. This targeted approach will boost your credibility and trustworthiness as an influencer, making your social media presence even more attractive to potential brand partners. Furthermore, ChatGPT's sentiment analysis capabilities can help you identify any potential red flags in your audience's perception of your brand collaborations. This enables you to address issues proactively and make necessary adjustments to maintain the authenticity and appeal of your content, ensuring the continued success of your social media presence.

Ask, "How can ChatGPT's sentiment analysis capabilities assist me in identifying the types of content and brand collaborations that resonate with my audience and boost my credibility as an influencer?" or "What guidance can ChatGPT offer in identifying and addressing potential red flags in my audience's perception of my brand collaborations to maintain the authenticity and appeal of my content?"

In summary, leveraging ChatGPT for sentiment analysis is a game-changer for anyone aiming to become a real powerhouse through social media. The insights you gain from understanding your audience's sentiment will empower you to make data-driven decisions that optimize your content and brand partnerships. With ChatGPT on your side, you can fine-tune your social media presence and maximize your revenue potential, bringing you one step closer to your millionaire dreams.

Adapting and refining your social media strategy

In the fast-paced world of social media, adaptability is crucial for those striving to become the best in the industry. As the landscape evolves, you need to refine your strategies to stay ahead of the curve and maximize your revenue potential. ChatGPT is the perfect tool to help you adapt and optimize your social media strategy, ensuring your continued success and income growth.

ChatGPT's ability to analyze vast amounts of data and identify emerging trends makes it an invaluable ally in your quest to become a social media millionaire. By leveraging this cutting-edge AI, you can uncover new tactics and opportunities for growth, helping you stay ahead of your competition and keep your finger on the pulse of the latest trends.

Just ask ChatGPT, "How can ChatGPT assist me in adapting and optimizing my social media strategy to stay ahead of the curve and maximize my revenue potential?" or "What are the key components of a successful social media strategy that I can refine with ChatGPT's help to ensure my continued success and income growth?"

Picture this: ChatGPT identifies an up-and-coming trend in your niche that has the potential to skyrocket your social media presence. Armed with this knowledge, you can create content that capitalizes on this trend, boosting your engagement rates and unlocking new monetization opportunities. With ChatGPT's support, you can continually refine your social media strategy, ensuring your brand remains relevant and your income keeps growing. Moreover, ChatGPT can help you optimize your social media strategy by analyzing the performance of your content and brand partnerships. By providing actionable insights, ChatGPT enables you to make data-driven decisions to improve your social media presence, whether it's adjusting your content mix or reevaluating your brand collaborations.

Try asking, "How can I use ChatGPT to uncover new tactics and opportunities for growth in my niche, helping me stay ahead of my competition and capitalize on emerging trends?" or "What insights can ChatGPT provide to help me optimize my content mix and brand collaborations based on the performance of my existing social media presence?"

In essence, using ChatGPT to adapt and refine your social media strategy is the key to unlocking your financial potential. By staying ahead of the curve and continuously optimizing your approach, you can unlock new opportunities for growth and monetization. With ChatGPT on your side, you'll have the tools and insights you need to solidify your social media success and generate the income you've always dreamed of.

Chapter 5: Online Course Creation and Sales

Identifying Your Course Niche and Target Audience

Selecting a profitable course niche

Choosing the right course niche is a game-changer for anyone who dreams of becoming a millionaire through online course creation. With the help of ChatGPT, you can tap into a goldmine of information and insights, enabling you to identify the most profitable course niche that aligns with your expertise and attracts a large, engaged audience.

Imagine having a powerful AI assistant that can analyze trends, popular search queries, and online discussions across various niches. ChatGPT does precisely that, providing you with invaluable data-driven insights to make informed decisions about your course niche. By leveraging ChatGPT's extensive knowledge database, you can identify high-demand areas with the potential for massive profitability.

Just ask, "How can ChatGPT help me identify the most profitable course niche that aligns with my expertise and has high market demand?" or "What kind of data and insights can ChatGPT provide to help me make informed decisions about the best course niche for my online course?"

Picture this scenario: You're an expert in a particular field, but you're unsure which topic within your field would be the most lucrative for your online course. With ChatGPT's assistance, you can uncover sub-niches and trending topics in high demand, ensuring that your course will have a broad appeal and a sizable target audience.

You can ask, "How can I use ChatGPT to uncover high-demand sub-niches and trending topics within my field of expertise, ensuring my online course will appeal to a broad audience?" or "What information can ChatGPT provide about my ideal target audience, including demographics, interests, and pain points, to help me create a successful online course and marketing campaign?"

But that's not all. ChatGPT can also help you identify your ideal target audience, which is crucial for your online course's success. By analyzing demographics, interests, and pain points, ChatGPT can provide you with a detailed understanding of the audience most likely to be interested in your course. This information is essential for creating tailored marketing campaigns and crafting course content that resonates with your audience, increasing your chances of making a significant income from your online course.

Understanding your target audience

If you're eager to become a entrepreneur through online course creation, having a deep understanding of your target audience is the key to unlocking massive revenue potential. Fortunately, ChatGPT is an exceptional tool that can help you gain insights into your audience's demographics, interests, and preferences, making your course a perfect fit for their needs.

Imagine having a crystal ball that can accurately predict your target audience's wants and needs. With ChatGPT, you can come incredibly close to achieving this level of insight. By conducting surveys or analyzing social media discussions, ChatGPT can provide you with valuable data that will enable you to tailor your course content and presentation to resonate with your intended audience.

For this, you can ask, "How can ChatGPT help me gain insights into my target audience's demographics, interests, and preferences to make my online course a perfect fit for their needs?" or "What are some methods ChatGPT can use to gather valuable data about my target audience to improve my online course content and presentation?"

By taking the time to understand your audience, you're setting yourself up for success. Higher engagement and satisfaction rates translate into more course sales, glowing reviews, and a reputation for excellence – all of which contribute to your journey towards becoming a millionaire. But the benefits don't stop there. Armed with the knowledge of your audience's preferences, you can create targeted marketing campaigns that speak directly of their needs and desires. This will increase conversion rates, driving even more sales and income from your online course.

You can easily ask, "How can ChatGPT help me gain insights into my target audience's demographics, interests, and preferences to make my online course a perfect fit for their needs?" or "What are some methods ChatGPT can use to gather valuable data about my target audience to improve my online course content and presentation?"

Moreover, ChatGPT's ability to analyze trends and online discussions can help you identify potential gaps in the market, which you can then fill with your expertly tailored course content. By addressing the unique needs of your target audience, you'll distinguish yourself from competitors and establish yourself as a thought leader in your niche.

Analyzing market demand and competition

Are you ready to dominate the online course market and pave your way to becoming a course creation wizard? Look no further than ChatGPT, your secret weapon to help you analyze market demand and competition in your chosen niche. By harnessing the power of ChatGPT, you'll have the edge you need to create an online course that stands out among the rest, ensuring long-term success and profitability.

In the world of online course creation, market research is crucial, and with ChatGPT's data analysis capabilities, you can conduct a thorough examination of existing courses in your niche. This will allow you to gauge their popularity and identify potential gaps in the market that you can capitalize on, creating a unique and irresistible course offering.

But the benefits of ChatGPT don't end there. As you dive deep into the competitive landscape, you'll gain invaluable insights into the strengths and weaknesses of your competitors. With this knowledge in hand, you'll be able to craft a course that not only fills market gaps but also outshines the competition in every way.

You can ask, "Discuss the importance of identifying your course niche and target audience in order to create an online course that caters to the specific needs and interests of your potential students." and "Explore the strategies you can use to pinpoint these aspects and how they contribute to the overall success of my course."

By positioning your course as a cut above the rest, you'll attract more students and generate higher revenues. ChatGPT's assistance in understanding the market and competition will help you stay ahead of the curve and continuously improve your course offerings, further solidifying your reputation as an industry leader.

The path to becoming a millionaire in the online course market is paved with strategic decisions and data-driven insights. With ChatGPT by your side, you'll have the support you need to navigate the competitive landscape, identify lucrative opportunities, and create a course that is both profitable and in high demand.

Developing High-Quality Course Content

Outlining your course structure and modules

Are you ready to create an online course that not only educates but also paves the way for your entrepreneurial dreams? Look no further than ChatGPT, the powerful tool that can help you outline your course structure and modules, ensuring a well-organized and comprehensive learning experience that students will love. Let's dive into the exciting world of course creation and explore how ChatGPT can revolutionize your content development process.

As you embark on your journey to create a high-quality online course, outlining the course structure and modules is a critical first step. ChatGPT is here to make that process smoother, faster, and more efficient. With its advanced capabilities, ChatGPT can help you brainstorm ideas, arrange topics logically, and develop a cohesive course outline that flows seamlessly from one module to the next.

A well-structured course is vital for student success, and successful students are the key to unlocking your potential as a millionaire course creator. By leveraging ChatGPT's expertise in generating outlines and structure suggestions, you'll save valuable time and ensure that your course content is both engaging and effective.

Just ask ChatGPT, "How can ChatGPT help me analyze market demand and competition in my chosen niche to create an online course that stands out and ensures long-term success and profitability?" or "What are some strategies ChatGPT can suggest for conducting thorough market research and identifying potential gaps in my chosen niche?"

But that's not all! ChatGPT can also help you identify areas for improvement within your course content, making recommendations to enhance the learning experience further. By utilizing these insights, you can refine your course material and deliver a truly exceptional product, setting you apart from the competition and maximizing your income potential.

In online course creation, the recipe for success includes a dash of innovation, a pinch of organization, and a healthy dose of cutting-edge technology like ChatGPT. By integrating ChatGPT into your content development process, you'll create a high-quality, well-structured course that delights your students and sets you on the fast track to achieving your financial dreams.

Just quickly ask, "How can I use ChatGPT to analyze the strengths and weaknesses of my competitors, so I can craft an online course that outshines the competition and fills market gaps?" or "What insights can ChatGPT provide to help me stay ahead of the curve and continuously improve my course offerings, solidifying my reputation as an industry leader in the online course market?"

In conclusion, ChatGPT is an indispensable tool for creating online courses that generate income and lead to long-term success. By harnessing the power of ChatGPT to develop well-organized and engaging course content, you'll be well on your way to securing your place among the elite ranks of course creators instead of just another average course maker.

Creating engaging lessons and materials

Are you ready to create an online course that not only educates but also has your bank account overflowing? Get ready to experience the incredible potential of ChatGPT, a powerful AI tool that can help you craft engaging lessons and materials. With ChatGPT on your side, you'll be well on your way to becoming a well-respected course creator. Let's dive into the exciting process of creating top-notch course content that keeps your students hooked and brings in the big bucks.

Creating high-quality lessons and materials is no easy feat, but ChatGPT's assistance makes the process significantly more manageable. ChatGPT can generate top-notch written content for your course, provide suggestions for real-world examples or case studies, and even help you craft quizzes and assessments to reinforce learning. By harnessing the power of ChatGPT, you can elevate your course materials to new heights, ensuring your students stay engaged and motivated throughout their learning journey.

Just ask, "What are the key elements of creating engaging lessons and materials for my online course, and how can ChatGPT help me achieve that?" or "How can I ensure my course content is captivating and appealing to my target audience, and what role can ChatGPT play in this process?"

The secret to skyrocketing your course sales lies in captivating course materials that result in higher completion rates and positive testimonials. When students rave about their experiences, word of mouth and glowing reviews will drive more sales and establish your course as a must-have resource. And as your sales increase, so does your income, bringing you closer to your visible millionaire dreams.

Use the prompt, "What specific techniques can ChatGPT provide to help me create quizzes and assessments that reinforce learning in my online course?" or "How can I use ChatGPT to continuously refine my course content based on feedback and the latest trends, ensuring my students' satisfaction and increased sales?"

But the benefits of ChatGPT don't stop there! By utilizing this cutting-edge AI tool, you can continually refine your course content, incorporating feedback and staying up to date with the latest trends and best practices. As you optimize your course materials, your students' satisfaction will soar, resulting in more referrals, increased sales, and ultimately, a fatter wallet.

Incorporating multimedia elements

Get ready to rev up your online course revenue by incorporating multimedia elements that not only engage your students but also set you on the path to becoming financially free. With the power of ChatGPT at your fingertips, you can create a course that caters to various learning styles and delivers an exceptional learning experience, ultimately boosting your income to new heights.

In the world of online course creation, incorporating multimedia elements is a surefire way to increase your course's appeal and effectiveness. ChatGPT can be a game-changer in this regard, helping you identify the most suitable multimedia elements to include in your course, such as videos, images, infographics, and interactive elements. By harnessing the creative capabilities of ChatGPT, you can design a rich and immersive learning experience that captivates your audience, resulting in higher satisfaction rates and word-of-mouth referrals.

Leveraging the advanced capabilities of the Open AI API, ChatGPT empowers you to create dynamic and engaging multimedia elements that cater to diverse learning styles. From generating captivating scripts for video content to offering suggestions for interactive quizzes, the Open AI API can serve as your creative partner throughout the course creation process. By utilizing this cutting-edge technology, you can ensure that your course remains up-to-date and appealing to a wide range of learners, further solidifying your position in the competitive online course market.

The key to unlocking extraordinary revenue from your online course is catering to different learning styles. By incorporating multimedia elements suggested by ChatGPT, you'll be able to engage visual, auditory, and kinesthetic learners, ensuring a broader appeal and higher completion rates. As your course becomes known for its comprehensive and engaging content, your sales will soar, bringing you one step closer to the kind of lifestyle you can only dream of now.

Just ask ChatGPT, "What strategies can ChatGPT suggest for engaging visual, auditory, and kinesthetic learners in my online course through multimedia elements?" or "How can I use ChatGPT to continually update and refine my multimedia content, ensuring my course stays ahead of the competition and maintains a steady stream of income?"

The potential of ChatGPT doesn't end there. By utilizing this advanced AI tool, you can continually update and refine your multimedia content, keeping your course fresh, relevant, and ahead of the competition. This commitment to quality will not only keep your students satisfied but also attract new learners, leading to a steady stream of income that grows over time.

Building Your Online Course Platform

Choosing the right course hosting platform

Attention, future millionaires! Selecting the perfect course hosting platform is paramount if you're looking to build an online course empire. With ChatGPT at your side, you can optimize your earning potential and ensure a smooth, seamless experience for your students – a critical step on your journey to wealth and success.

Choosing the right course hosting platform can make or break your online course venture. The ideal platform will provide the needed features, offer scalability as your business grows, and have competitive pricing. Enter ChatGPT: your secret weapon in researching and comparing different platforms, ensuring you find the best fit for your course requirements.

By leveraging the power of ChatGPT, you can efficiently and effectively evaluate various hosting platforms based on factors such as user experience, support, and integration capabilities. ChatGPT's ability to analyze massive amounts of data in real-time can help you make an informed choice, ensuring that you invest your resources wisely and set your online course business up for success.

Just ask for help like "What are the key factors I should consider when choosing a course hosting platform, and how can ChatGPT help me research and compare different platforms?" or "How can ChatGPT support me in finding the best fit for my specific course requirements when selecting a hosting platform?"

Imagine the possibilities! With the perfect course hosting platform, you can create a user-friendly, engaging, and accessible learning experience that attracts a broad audience. As your course gains traction, positive reviews and testimonials will start pouring in, driving even more students to your course, and propelling your revenue to new heights.

The magic doesn't stop there. With ChatGPT's ongoing support, you can continuously monitor the performance of your chosen platform and stay informed about any updates, new features, or changes in pricing. This vigilance will help you maintain a competitive edge and make any necessary adjustments to your course platform, ensuring long-term success and ever-increasing profits.

You can ask, "How can I use ChatGPT to evaluate various hosting platforms based on user experience, support, and integration capabilities, ensuring I invest my resources wisely?" or "What strategies can ChatGPT suggest for continuously monitoring the performance of my chosen course hosting platform and staying informed about updates, new features, or changes in pricing?"

Customizing your course website for user experience

Is key to retaining students and ensuring they complete the course. An intuitive, user-friendly, and visually appealing website attracts potential students and increases their likelihood of recommending your course to others.

ChatGPT can assist you in generating design ideas, crafting compelling website copy, and even offering suggestions for website structure and layout. By using ChatGPT to create an engaging and accessible website, you can boost your course's appeal, leading to higher enrollment rates and greater revenue generation.

Ask ChatGPT to help with, "What are the key elements of an engaging and user-friendly course website, and how can ChatGPT assist me in generating design ideas and crafting compelling website copy?" or "How can ChatGPT help me create an accessible website that increases my course's appeal, leading to higher enrollment rates and greater revenue generation?"

An exceptional course website is intuitive, visually appealing, and easy to navigate, ensuring that your students have a positive experience from start to finish. With ChatGPT's creative capabilities, you can generate innovative design ideas, craft compelling website copy, and even receive suggestions for website structure and layout. By harnessing the power of ChatGPT, you'll build an engaging and accessible website that skyrockets your course's appeal and keeps students coming back for more.

Imagine the possibilities! With an outstanding course website, you can create an immersive and satisfying learning experience that generates buzz and word-of-mouth referrals. As your course's reputation grows, so does your student base – and with it, your income. You'll be well on your way to achieving those millions as more and more students flock to your online course, eager to learn and share their experiences with others.

You can just ask it to help you easily using, "In what ways can ChatGPT help me generate innovative design ideas, craft compelling website copy, and receive suggestions for website structure and layout to create an outstanding course website?" or "How can I utilize ChatGPT to monitor my website's performance, analyze user behavior and feedback, and make data-driven decisions to continuously improve the user experience and maximize my course website's effectiveness?"

But it doesn't end there. ChatGPT can also help you monitor your website's performance and identify areas for improvement. By regularly analyzing user behavior and feedback, you can make data-driven decisions that enhance the user experience and maximize the effectiveness of your course website. This commitment to continuous improvement will ensure that your online course business remains competitive and profitable in the long run.

Integrating ChatGPT for learner support and interaction

Integrating ChatGPT into your online course platform is a game-changing move that can catapult you to millionaire status. By offering personalized assistance, answering FAQs, and providing real-time feedback on assignments, you'll significantly enhance your students' experience and satisfaction with your course.

Improved student engagement is one of the major advantages of using ChatGPT. When learners feel supported and receive timely assistance, they're more likely to stay engaged, complete the course, and leave positive reviews. This, in turn, boosts your course's reputation and attracts more students, driving up your income potential.

Imagine the edge you'll have over competitors as you seamlessly offer AI-driven learner support that's both efficient and effective. Your students will appreciate the personalized attention they receive, and as word spreads about the exceptional learning experience you provide, you'll see an increase in enrollments and revenue.

Just ask, "How can I best integrate ChatGPT into my online course platform to provide personalized assistance, answer FAQs, and offer real-time feedback on assignments, enhancing my students' experience and satisfaction?" or "What are the key benefits of using ChatGPT for learner support and interaction, and how can this integration help me boost my course's reputation and increase my income potential?"

Furthermore, ChatGPT's integration can help foster a sense of community among your students. With AI-powered discussion forums and chat features, learners can connect, share ideas, and solve problems collaboratively. This social aspect improves the overall learning experience and encourages students to recommend your course to their peers, resulting in even more revenue for your online course business.

Another key benefit of using ChatGPT is the ability to scale your support and interaction without increasing your workload. As your course grows in popularity and your student base expands, ChatGPT's AI capabilities will enable you to maintain a high level of learner support without additional staff or resources. This means you can maximize your profits while maintaining a top-notch learning experience for your students.

You can ask ChatGPT, "How can I leverage ChatGPT's capabilities to create AI-powered discussion forums and chat features that foster a sense of community among my students, ultimately leading to more course recommendations and increased revenue?" or "What strategies can I use to scale my learner support and interaction using ChatGPT as my course grows in popularity, allowing me to maintain a high level of learner support without additional staff or resources?"

Integrating ChatGPT into your online course platform is an investment that will pay off in spades. By harnessing the power of AI for personalized learner support and interaction, you'll foster a learning environment that keeps students engaged, satisfied, and eager to spread the word about your course. The result? A thriving online course business that brings you ever closer to that coveted millionaire status.

Marketing and Promoting Your Online Course

Developing a comprehensive marketing strategy

Crafting a marketing strategy that drives traffic, conversions, and profitability is essential for your online course business. With ChatGPT by your side, you can unlock the secrets to attracting students and generating revenue like a true millionaire.

Harnessing the power of ChatGPT enables you to identify promotional opportunities and brainstorm marketing ideas tailored to your target audience. Whether you're exploring social media advertising, content marketing, or influencer partnerships, ChatGPT can help you pinpoint the most effective channels to reach potential students.

Just ask, "How can I use ChatGPT to identify the best promotional opportunities and marketing ideas tailored to my target audience, driving traffic, conversions, and profitability for my online course business?" or "What are the key components of a successful marketing strategy for my online course, and how can ChatGPT assist me in creating a plan that maximizes visibility and reach?"

But the benefits of ChatGPT don't stop there. This AI-driven tool can create a detailed marketing plan for your online course, allowing you to set clear goals and track your progress. By leveraging ChatGPT's capabilities, you can stay on top of your marketing efforts, making data-driven decisions that maximize your course's visibility and reach.

Imagine the advantage you'll have over competitors as you tap into ChatGPT's creative genius to craft compelling ad copy, persuasive email campaigns and engaging social media content. Your online course will stand out from the crowd, capturing the attention of potential students and converting them into loyal, paying customers.

It only takes the following, "How can I leverage ChatGPT's creative capabilities to craft compelling ad copy, persuasive email campaigns, and engaging social media content that sets my online course apart from competitors and attracts potential students?" or "As my course gains traction and my student base grows, what strategies can I use with ChatGPT to refine my marketing strategy, capitalize on emerging trends, and ensure the long-term success of my online course business?"

As your course gains traction and your student base grows, ChatGPT will continue to be an invaluable resource, helping you refine your marketing strategy and capitalize on emerging trends. The result? A thriving online course business that brings in the big bucks.

Leveraging ChatGPT to create persuasive sales copy

When it comes to making bank in the world of online course creation, the secret sauce is persuasive sales copy that captivates your target audience. That's where ChatGPT comes in, turbocharging your sales copy and turning potential students into paying customers.

By tapping into ChatGPT's natural language generation capabilities, you can create magnetic copy for your course landing page, promotional emails, and advertisements that showcase your course's unique selling points. Think of ChatGPT as your personal copywriting guru, helping you craft a compelling message that resonates with your audience and drives course sign-ups.

Just ask, "How can I use ChatGPT's natural language generation capabilities to craft magnetic sales copy that showcases my course's unique selling points and captivates my target audience?" or "What are the key elements of persuasive sales copy, and how can ChatGPT assist me in developing compelling messaging that drives course sign-ups and revenue?"

As you unleash the power of ChatGPT, your sales copy becomes an unstoppable force, effortlessly communicating the value of your course and convincing potential students that they cannot miss out on what you have to offer. And as more students enroll on your course, your revenue starts to soar, bringing you closer to that millionaire status you've been dreaming of.

But wait, there's more! ChatGPT continues beyond just crafting persuasive sales copy. It can also help you tweak and refine your messaging based on user feedback and market trends. This means you can stay ahead of the curve and adapt your sales copy to resonate with your audience even more, further increasing your course's appeal and profitability.

Supercharge your prompts with "How can I utilize ChatGPT to tweak and refine my sales copy based on user feedback and market trends, ensuring that my messaging stays relevant and appealing to my target audience?" or "What strategies can I use with ChatGPT to continuously improve my sales copy, further increasing my course's appeal and profitability in the competitive world of online course creation?"

So, get ready to embark on a wild ride to being a millionaire, as ChatGPT supercharges your sales copy like a high-powered, overclocked gaming rig. With ChatGPT by your side, there's no limit to the success you can achieve in the world of online course creation. Hold on tight because you're about to enter the stratosphere of revenue generation!

Utilizing social media, email marketing, and partnerships

When it comes to skyrocketing your online course revenue and reaching that millionaire throne, combining the power of social media, email marketing, and partnerships with the prowess of ChatGPT is like strapping a jet engine to a rocket. Prepare for liftoff!

ChatGPT, the ultimate AI-powered tool, can help you craft captivating content for your social media posts, drawing potential students to your course like moths to a flame. It can optimize your email campaigns, ensuring that your message is not only heard but also compels your audience to act. And when it comes to partnerships, ChatGPT's got your back, helping you identify the perfect collaborators to expand your reach and drive more traffic to your course.

Just ask, "How can I use ChatGPT to create captivating social media content that attracts potential students and increases my online course's visibility?" or "What strategies can ChatGPT help me develop for optimizing my email marketing campaigns and driving more course sign-ups?"

With ChatGPT in your corner, you'll quickly become a marketing maestro, pulling all the right levers to reach the pinnacle of online course success. Watch in awe as your audience grows and your course enrollment soars, bringing you closer to that coveted millionaire milestone.

You can happily ask, "How can ChatGPT assist me in identifying suitable partners or collaborators to expand my reach and drive more traffic to my online course?" or "What insights and recommendations can ChatGPT provide to help me refine and adapt my marketing strategies based on the ever-changing digital landscape, ensuring my online course remains competitive?"

And as you ride the wave of success, ChatGPT remains by your side, helping you to refine and adapt your marketing strategies based on the ever-changing digital landscape. This means you'll always be one step ahead of the game, ensuring your online course remains a powerhouse in your niche.

Pricing and Monetization Strategies

Determining the ideal pricing model for your course

In the quest to be the best in the course industry, choosing the perfect pricing model for your online course is like finding the golden key to the treasure chest. And guess what? ChatGPT is your treasure map, guiding you through the maze of pricing options to unlock the full potential of your e-learning empire.

With ChatGPT at your side, you'll evaluate various pricing models, from one-time fees and subscriptions to tiered pricing, like a seasoned pro. Analyzing market trends and competitor pricing becomes a breeze, and you'll pinpoint the ideal pricing strategy that aligns with your target audience and course content. ChatGPT's invaluable insights and recommendations will be your secret weapon in setting a competitive, profitable price that catapults your course to the top of the leaderboard.

Just ask your new digital buddy, "How can ChatGPT help me evaluate various pricing models, such as one-time fees, subscriptions, and tiered pricing, to find the best fit for my online course?" or "What insights can ChatGPT provide on the market trends and competitor pricing to assist me in setting a competitive and profitable price for my course?"

As you watch the revenue roll in, don't forget that ChatGPT can also help you optimize your pricing over time. Market conditions change, and so do your competitors. Still, with ChatGPT's data-driven insights, you'll always stay ahead of the curve, ready to adapt and evolve your pricing strategy for maximum impact.

Now, let's wrap things up with a tech-geeky twist: choosing the right pricing model for your online course is like selecting the most efficient algorithm to solve a complex problem. With ChatGPT as your trusty assistant, you'll quickly crack the code, unlocking the riches that await in the world of e-learning. So, get ready to ride the wave of success, because with ChatGPT, you're not only a course creator, but also a master of monetization. To infinity and beyond!

Try asking, "How can ChatGPT help me optimize my pricing strategy over time, taking into account changing market conditions and competitor activities?" or "What data-driven insights can ChatGPT offer to ensure my pricing strategy remains effective and adaptable in the ever-evolving e-learning landscape?"

Exploring additional monetization opportunities

Picture yourself as an e-learning entrepreneur, seeking to uncover hidden revenue streams and transform your online course into a million-dollar goldmine. The secret to this treasure hunt lies in exploring additional monetization opportunities, and ChatGPT is your trusty sidekick, ready to help you unearth these lucrative gems.

With ChatGPT's assistance, you can discover upselling, cross-selling, and affiliate marketing opportunities that seamlessly align with your course content and audience needs. Imagine offering your students exclusive access to premium content, advanced tools, or complementary courses – all with the goal of boosting your bottom line.

You can quickly get a good response by asking, "How can ChatGPT help me identify upselling, cross-selling, and affiliate marketing opportunities that align with my online course and audience needs?" or "What recommendations can ChatGPT provide for creating premium content, advanced tools, or complementary courses to boost my bottom line?"

By leveraging ChatGPT's suggestions and insights, you're not only creating added value for your students but also unlocking new pathways to revenue generation. As you capitalize on these opportunities, watch your e-learning business grow and flourish like a well-tended money tree.

As we bring this treasure hunt to a close, let's remember that unlocking these additional revenue streams is like discovering a secret bonus level in a video game. With ChatGPT as your trusty game guide, you'll level up your e-learning business, racking up points and high scores in the form of increased profits. So, buckle up and get ready to embark on a thrilling adventure to the land of e-learning riches, where your million-dollar dreams await! Game on!

Leverage ChatGPT with, "How can I leverage ChatGPT's insights to create added value for my students while unlocking new revenue streams for my e-learning business?" or "What strategies and tips can ChatGPT offer to help me level up my online course business and maximize my profits from additional monetization opportunities?"

Offering discounts and incentives to boost sales

Ready to skyrocket your online course sales to the financial stratosphere? Offering discounts and incentives could be your winning formula, and with ChatGPT by your side, you'll design promotional campaigns that resonate with your target audience like never before.

Harness the power of ChatGPT to create a sense of urgency with limited time offers that will have students scrambling to enroll. Or tap into the magic of seasonal discounts that make your course the must-have gift for learners during holidays and special occasions.

Just ask, "How can ChatGPT help me design promotional campaigns that create a sense of urgency and resonate with my target audience?" or "What suggestions does ChatGPT have for creating seasonal discounts or limited time offers that will boost my online course sales?"

But why stop there? ChatGPT can also help you devise referral programs that turn your students into brand ambassadors. Imagine the power of your students sharing your course with their networks, and the snowball effect it creates as more and more people discover your content. With ChatGPT's expertise in crafting persuasive promotions, you'll drive enrollment numbers to new heights, maximizing your course revenue and inching closer to that independent living dream.

You can quickly ask, "How can ChatGPT assist me in devising a successful referral program that turns my students into brand ambassadors and drives course enrollments?" or "What strategies and tips can ChatGPT offer for crafting persuasive promotions to maximize my online course revenue and achieve my millionaire dreams?"

As we wrap up this thrilling ride, remember that with ChatGPT's assistance, you're not just offering discounts and incentives, you're unlocking the vault to online course riches. So put on your captain's hat and set sail towards a treasure island overflowing with students and revenue, because with ChatGPT as your first mate, your e-learning empire is destined to rule the seven seas of success. Ahoy, matey!

Course Evaluation and Improvement

Collecting Feedback from Learners

Collecting feedback from learners is essential for ensuring the ongoing success and improvement of your online course. By gathering insights on the strengths and weaknesses of your course content and delivery, you can make informed decisions on areas that require refinement.

ChatGPT can help you design effective feedback forms and surveys and analyze the responses to identify patterns and trends. Incorporating student feedback into your course development process can create a more valuable learning experience, leading to increased student satisfaction and higher revenue potential.

You can easily ask ChatGPT, "How can ChatGPT help me design effective feedback forms and surveys that will gather valuable insights from my learners?" or "What are the best strategies for identifying the strengths and weaknesses of my online course based on the feedback collected?"

If you're ready to turn your online course into a revenue-generating powerhouse, collecting feedback from learners is the key that unlocks a treasure trove of potential improvements. ChatGPT is the perfect sidekick to help you gather those insights and refine your course like a master craftsman.

Design effective feedback forms and surveys with ChatGPT's assistance, ensuring you capture the most valuable information from your students. Then, let ChatGPT work its magic to analyze the responses, identifying patterns and trends that will inform your next course of action.

Just ask, "How can ChatGPT assist me in analyzing the feedback responses and identifying patterns and trends to improve my course content and delivery?" or "What recommendations does ChatGPT have for incorporating student feedback into my course development process to increase student satisfaction and revenue potential?"

It's not just about collecting feedback; it's about putting it to work for you. With ChatGPT's guidance, you'll transform your course into a learning experience that resonates with students, leading to increased satisfaction and loyalty. And as we all know, happy students are more likely to spread the word about your course, driving more enrollments and fattening up your bank account.

Using ChatGPT to analyze course performance

Using ChatGPT to analyze course performance involves leveraging the AI's analytical capabilities to evaluate various aspects of your e-learning business, such as student engagement, completion rates, and overall revenue. ChatGPT can process large volumes of data quickly and provides you with actionable insights to optimize your course offerings.

By using ChatGPT to identify areas of improvement, you can enhance the quality and effectiveness of your online course, ultimately leading to higher student retention and increased revenue. Picture this: your online course is a well-oiled machine, and ChatGPT is the master mechanic that keeps it running at peak performance. By using ChatGPT to analyze course performance, you can rev up your e-learning business and set your sights on those millionaire dreams!

Just ask, "How can ChatGPT help me analyze student engagement, completion rates, and overall revenue to optimize my course offerings?" or "What are the best strategies for using ChatGPT's analytical capabilities to evaluate the effectiveness of my online course and identify areas of improvement?"

ChatGPT's analytical prowess is just what you need to dive into the nitty-gritty of student engagement, completion rates, and revenue generation. With a keen eye on the data, ChatGPT can identify areas where your course can be fine-tuned for even greater success. So let ChatGPT work its magic, highlighting the path to higher student retention and increased revenue. Armed with these insights, you'll be able to optimize your course offerings like a pro, transforming your e-learning business into a force to be reckoned with.

You can easily ask, "How can I use ChatGPT to fine-tune my course for greater success in terms of student retention and increased revenue?" or "What recommendations does ChatGPT have for optimizing my course offerings based on its analysis of course performance and data trends?"

And as you embrace ChatGPT's guidance and watch your online course soar to new heights, don't forget to celebrate your achievements. Pop the champagne and let out a triumphant "Eureka!" because, with ChatGPT by your side, your bulging bank accounts is well within reach. To infinity and beyond, e-learning tycoon!

Implementing updates and refinements

Implementing updates and refinements is crucial for maintaining the relevance and value of your online course. ChatGPT can assist you in identifying necessary updates to your course content, instructional methods, or multimedia elements, ensuring that your students receive the best possible learning experience.

Additionally, ChatGPT can help you prioritize these updates based on their potential impact on student satisfaction and revenue generation. By continually refining your course offerings and adapting to the needs of your audience, you can stay ahead of the competition and maximize your earnings in the e-learning market.

Just ask ChatGPT to help with the following, "What specific updates and refinements should I consider for my online course to maintain its relevance and value for students?" or "How can ChatGPT help me identify areas of my course that need improvement in terms of content, instructional methods, or multimedia elements?"

If you're ready to skyrocket your online course earnings and join the ranks of e-learning millionaires, look no further than ChatGPT. With its sharp insights, ChatGPT is your secret weapon for refining your course and keeping it fresh, ensuring your students are always engaged and eager to learn. By implementing updates and refinements in your course content, instructional methods, or multimedia elements, you can keep your students coming back for more. And with ChatGPT's guidance, you can prioritize these updates based on their potential impact on student satisfaction and revenue generation.

Don't settle for a stagnant course offering. Embrace the power of ChatGPT and stay ahead of the competition, adapting to the ever-changing needs of your audience. As you continually refine your course, you'll see your earnings in the e-learning market soar, bringing you closer and closer to those coveted millionaire dreams.

To help, use, "What strategies can ChatGPT suggest for prioritizing updates based on their potential impact on student satisfaction and revenue generation?" or "How can I use ChatGPT's insights to adapt my course to the ever-changing needs of my audience and stay ahead of the competition in the e-learning market?"

Now, it's time to act! Roll up your sleeves and dive into the world of updates and refinements with ChatGPT by your side. As you watch your online course transform, remember this mantra: adapt, refine, and conquer! So, buckle up, e-learning entrepreneur, and let's ride this rocket to e-learning superstardom!

Chapter 6: E-commerce and Generating Product Descriptions

Understanding the Importance of Descriptions

The Role of product descriptions in driving sales

Welcome to the world of e-commerce, where the perfect product description can propel your store into the millionaire's club! With the help of ChatGPT, you can create powerful, persuasive product descriptions that captivate customers and persuade them to open their wallets.

A well-crafted product description is like a salesperson, highlighting a product's unique selling points and benefits, making it irresistible to potential customers. Your descriptions must be compelling, informative, and tailored to your target audience. And that's where ChatGPT comes in, working its AI magic to generate exceptional descriptions that drive sales sky-high. Forget about generic, run-of-the-mill descriptions that leave customers unimpressed. Instead, tap into ChatGPT's potential to create captivating content that showcases your products in the best light, increasing the perceived value and pushing customers to complete their purchases. The result? A skyrocketing revenue that brings you closer and closer to your millionaire dreams.

Just simply ask, "How can I use ChatGPT to generate compelling, informative, and audience-targeted product descriptions that will drive sales for my e-commerce store?" or "What are some best practices and key elements ChatGPT can incorporate into product descriptions to increase the perceived value of my products and encourage customers to complete their purchases?"

So, what are you waiting for? Harness the power of ChatGPT to create those million-dollar product descriptions, and watch as your e-commerce store becomes a sales powerhouse! Keep pushing those boundaries, and remember with the right AI-generated descriptions, the sky's the limit!

Crafting descriptions that resonate with your target audience

Get ready to watch your e-commerce profits soar as you discover the secret to crafting product descriptions that truly resonate with your target audience. Say goodbye to generic content and hello to highly customized, engaging descriptions that speak directly to your customers' hearts and wallets.

ChatGPT is your ticket to unlocking the full potential of audience-focused product descriptions. By understanding your customers' preferences, pain points, and aspirations, you can generate content that addresses their needs and expectations. ChatGPT helps you create descriptions that showcase your products and forge a genuine connection with your audience. Imagine the impact on your bottom line as your customers feel seen and understood, driving them to make purchases confidently. This is the power of highly targeted product descriptions, and with ChatGPT by your side, you're on the fast track to e-commerce success.

You can just type, "How can ChatGPT help me understand my target audience's preferences, pain points, and aspirations to create highly customized product descriptions that address their needs and expectations?" or "What strategies can I use with ChatGPT to generate audience-focused product descriptions that showcase my products, forge genuine connections, and ultimately drive more sales for my e-commerce store?"

The future of e-commerce belongs to those who can master the art of captivating their audience. Embrace the power of ChatGPT, and watch your profits skyrocket, catapulting you closer to your financially free goal. Get ready for takeoff, and remember with ChatGPT, your e-commerce success story is just a few well-crafted descriptions away!

The impact of SEO and keyword optimization in product descriptions

Search engine optimization (SEO) is a vital component of a successful e-commerce strategy, as it helps your products rank higher in search results, driving more organic traffic to your store. By incorporating relevant keywords and optimizing your product descriptions, you can increase their visibility and attract potential customers actively searching for products like yours.

ChatGPT can aid in identifying and integrating appropriate keywords into your descriptions, ensuring that your content is engaging and SEO-friendly, ultimately leading to increased sales and revenue. Let's dive into SEO and keyword optimization in product descriptions, a critical component of your e-commerce empire. Unlock the power of search engine optimization and watch your online store skyrocket the search rankings, bringing a flood of organic traffic and eager customers.

You can ask ChatGPT, "How can ChatGPT help me identify relevant keywords and optimize my product descriptions for improved search engine rankings and increased organic traffic?" or "What are some best practices for incorporating keywords into product descriptions using ChatGPT while maintaining engaging and compelling content?"

ChatGPT is your secret weapon for creating SEO-optimized product descriptions that hit the sweet spot between engaging content and search engine visibility. By identifying and seamlessly integrating relevant keywords into your descriptions, ChatGPT ensures that your e-commerce store stands out in the vast search results, attracting customers actively searching for products like yours.

Imagine the thrill of watching your sales and revenue soar as your products consistently rank higher in search results, drawing in a steady stream of potential buyers. This is the power of SEO and keyword optimization in product descriptions, and with ChatGPT's assistance, your millionaire dreams are well within reach.

You can ask, "How can I use ChatGPT to track the impact of SEO and keyword optimization on my product descriptions and measure the increase in sales and revenue as a result?" or "What strategies can I employ with ChatGPT to stay ahead of the competition and maintain high search rankings for my e-commerce store in the long run?"

So, gear up for the e-commerce success you've always envisioned. Embrace the power of ChatGPT and let your SEO-optimized product descriptions propel you towards those above average entrepreneurial visions. The sky's the limit, and with ChatGPT, you're ready to soar.

Leveraging ChatGPT for E-commerce Content

Generating persuasive and engaging product descriptions

ChatGPT's powerful AI capabilities can be harnessed to create persuasive and engaging product descriptions that capture the attention of potential customers. By providing a few key inputs about your product, ChatGPT can generate descriptions that highlight its features, benefits, and unique selling points compellingly.

This results in content that informs and educates customers and persuades them to make a purchase, ultimately contributing to your e-commerce store's profitability. Picture this: your e-commerce store has product descriptions that resonate with your audience, persuading them to hit that 'Add to Cart confidently' button. Thanks to ChatGPT, generating these compelling and engaging descriptions has never been easier.

Just ask, "How can I effectively use ChatGPT to generate product descriptions that emphasize key features, benefits, and unique selling points in a persuasive manner?" or "What tips and strategies can ChatGPT offer to create engaging content that informs and educates customers while encouraging them to make a purchase?"

By simply feeding ChatGPT some essential information about your product, the AI gets to work crafting descriptions that emphasize the features, benefits, and unique selling points that matter most to your customers. This leads to content that not only informs but also convinces them to buy, transforming your e-commerce store into a profit-generating powerhouse.

With ChatGPT by your side, you can create irresistible product descriptions at lightning speed, leaving you more time to focus on other aspects of your e-commerce empire. As your descriptions work their magic, your store's profitability will soar, driving you ever closer to that destiny calling millionaire milestone.

You can try asking, "How can I streamline the process of generating numerous product descriptions using ChatGPT without sacrificing quality or personalization for my e-commerce store?" or "What methods can ChatGPT recommend for tracking the performance of my product descriptions and making improvements over time to increase my store's profitability?"

As you take your e-commerce business to new heights, don't forget to celebrate the role that ChatGPT has played in supercharging your product descriptions. So, raise a glass to the AI-powered revolution in e-commerce content, and toast to your future success. Cheers!

Utilizing ChatGPT for keyword research and optimization

Keyword research and optimization are essential to crafting effective product descriptions that rank well in search engine results. ChatGPT can help you identify the most relevant and high-performing keywords related to your products, which can be incorporated into your descriptions to enhance their SEO value.

By optimizing your content with the right keywords, you can increase your store's visibility and attract more organic traffic, leading to higher sales and greater revenue generation. Picture your e-commerce store skyrocketing to the top of search engine results, drawing in hordes of organic traffic ready to buy. With ChatGPT's prowess in keyword research and optimization, this dream can become a reality.

Just type the following, "How can I use ChatGPT to identify the most relevant and high-performing keywords for my products to improve my e-commerce store's search engine rankings?" or "What strategies can ChatGPT recommend for incorporating keywords into my product descriptions without making them sound forced or unnatural?"

Harnessing the power of ChatGPT, you can identify the most relevant, high-performing keywords for your products. Seamlessly incorporate these gems into your descriptions to boost their SEO value and watch your store's visibility soar. More visibility means more organic traffic, which ultimately translates to higher sales and greater revenue generation. Imagine the thrill of seeing your e-commerce store rise through the ranks, outshining competitors as you claim your spot among the millionaire elite. ChatGPT is your secret weapon in this quest for e-commerce dominance, making your keyword optimization game stronger than ever.

You can easily ask, "How can ChatGPT help me analyze the performance of my keyword-optimized product descriptions and suggest improvements to enhance my e-commerce store's visibility further?" or "How can I use ChatGPT to create a WordPress plugin that allows me to create product descriptions in bulk based on the title and attributes of the product?"

As you revel in the success of your e-commerce empire, spare a moment to acknowledge the AI-powered genius of ChatGPT. It's been an invaluable partner in your ascent to millionaire status. So, give a nod to the tech that helped you get there – and then, put on your shades, because your e-commerce future is looking bright.

Streamlining the content creation process with AI assistance

You can turbocharge your product description writing process, saving you precious time and effort. No more grinding away at crafting compelling descriptions – let ChatGPT do the heavy lifting.

Unleash the power of ChatGPT to generate engaging and optimized content at lightning speed, leaving you free to focus on other crucial aspects of your business, like marketing and customer service. The efficiency gained from AI technology translates to cost savings, boosting your profits and bringing you closer to being a top e-commerce millionaire. Picture yourself sailing through the content creation process with ease, thanks to ChatGPT. While your competitors struggle to keep up, you'll be miles ahead, reaping the rewards of your AI-driven e-commerce strategy. The road to e-commerce success has never been smoother.

Just ask ChatGPT, "How can I efficiently utilize ChatGPT to generate high-quality and engaging product descriptions that resonate with my target audience and encourage them to make a purchase?" or "What are some best practices for collaborating with ChatGPT to ensure my product descriptions are not only well-written but also optimized for search engines to increase my e-commerce store's visibility and organic traffic?"

Enhancing Product Presentation

Incorporating high-quality images and videos

Get ready to level up your e-commerce game with exceptional product presentation! By incorporating high-quality images and videos, you're setting yourself up for a significant boost in sales. Customers love to see what they're buying, and having top-notch visuals can make all the difference between a hesitant shopper and a confident buyer.

Now, here's where ChatGPT comes into play: It can help you create captivating scripts for product videos and provide valuable recommendations on presenting your products in images. That's right – ChatGPT has got your back in the world of product presentation, making your journey to millionaire status even smoother. Imagine your e-commerce store dazzling customers with stunning visuals, thanks to the expert guidance of ChatGPT. You'll be raking in sales like never before, and your competitors will be left in the dust, wondering how you managed to create such an alluring online shopping experience.

Just ask, "How can I use ChatGPT to create engaging and persuasive scripts for product videos that showcase the unique features and benefits of my products?" or "What recommendations can ChatGPT provide to help me present my products effectively in images, so my e-commerce store stands out from the competition and appeals to potential customers?"

So, what are you waiting for? Harness the power of ChatGPT and watch as your e-commerce empire flourishes. Remember, the key to unlocking a fortune lies in the details – and with ChatGPT by your side, you've got every detail covered. Get ready to soar to new heights, and while you're at it, give a friendly wave to your competition down below!

Creating visual elements using ChatGPT's support

ChatGPT's versatile AI capabilities can also be utilized to create captivating visual elements for your e-commerce store. ChatGPT can help generate ideas for images, infographics, and other visual content that can enhance your product presentation by providing inputs on the desired theme, style, and key features of your product.

These visuals make your store more visually appealing and help convey important information about your products in an easily digestible format, increasing the likelihood of customers purchasing. Ready to make a splash in the world of e-commerce? Dive into the world of visuals and let ChatGPT be your guide! With ChatGPT's support, you can create show-stopping visual elements to make your e-commerce store stand out from the crowd. Watch as your store transforms into a visual wonderland, attracting customers from far and wide!

Just ask the amazing ChatGPT, "What kind of visual elements can ChatGPT help me generate to improve the overall look and feel of my e-commerce store based on my product's theme, style, and key features?" or "How can I use ChatGPT to create infographics that showcase the most important information about my products in a visually appealing and easily digestible manner?"

By leveraging ChatGPT's AI capabilities, you'll have access to a treasure trove of ideas for images, infographics, and other visual content. Just provide your desired theme, style, and key product features, and

ChatGPT will generate eye-catching concepts that can be used to enhance your product presentation. These visuals not only elevate your store's aesthetic appeal but also convey crucial information about your products in an engaging, easy-to-understand format.

As you revolutionize your e-commerce store with ChatGPT's guidance, you'll be paving your way to millionaire success. Customers will be drawn to your store like moths to a flame, dazzled by the stunning visual elements that set you apart from the competition. And with every purchase they make, you'll be one step closer to achieving your financial dreams.

Just ask, "What specific ideas can ChatGPT provide to help me create unique and engaging visual content that will attract customers to my e-commerce store and set me apart from my competitors?" or "How can I use ChatGPT's AI capabilities to optimize my e-commerce store's visual elements, ensuring they effectively convey crucial product information and contribute to my financial success?"

So, gear up and get ready to ride the ChatGPT wave to e-commerce stardom! And while you're at it, remember to take a moment to enjoy the view from the top, as you leave your competitors in your wake. After all, the future of e-commerce belongs to those who dare to dream big and embrace the power of AI!

Balancing text and visuals for optimal user experience

Achieving the right balance between text and visuals is crucial for delivering an optimal user experience on your e-commerce store. Too much text can overwhelm customers, while too few visuals can leave them wanting more information about your products.

ChatGPT can assist in finding this balance by providing guidance on the appropriate amount of text and visuals for each product description. By optimizing your product presentation, you can create a more engaging shopping experience for your customers, leading to increased sales and higher profits. Step right up, future millionaires! Unlock the secret to e-commerce success by striking the perfect balance between text and visuals on your online store. With ChatGPT by your side, you'll craft a delightful shopping experience that keeps customers returning for more.

You can easily ask, "How can I use ChatGPT to determine the ideal balance between text and visuals for my e-commerce product descriptions to enhance user experience and boost sales?" or "What guidelines or suggestions can ChatGPT provide for creating engaging product descriptions that effectively combine text and visuals?"

Avoid drowning your customers in a sea of text; don't leave them high and dry with too few visuals. ChatGPT can help you find that sweet spot, ensuring that your product descriptions are informative and visually engaging. No more guesswork, just a seamless fusion of text and visuals that will have customers reaching for their wallets. As your sales soar and your profits skyrocket, you'll wonder how you managed without ChatGPT. Your e-commerce store will transform into a well-oiled machine, churning out perfectly balanced product presentations that keep customers hooked. And with every purchase, you'll inch closer to being on top in this industry.

Just ask ChatGPT, "Can ChatGPT help me identify the most effective product presentation strategies to keep my customers engaged and increase the likelihood of making a purchase?" or "How can I use ChatGPT's insights to optimize my e-commerce store's product presentations, ensuring they appeal to my target audience and contribute to my overall success?"

So, what are you waiting for? Harness the power of ChatGPT and take your e-commerce game to the next level. Remember, the path to e-commerce domination is paved with the perfect balance of text and visuals. And as you bask in your success, don't forget to share your secret weapon, ChatGPT, with the world. After all, every e-commerce mogul needs a trusty sidekick!

Optimizing Your E-commerce Store for Conversion

Implementing user-friendly website design and navigation

Creating a user-friendly e-commerce store with an intuitive design and easy navigation is crucial for ensuring a seamless shopping experience for your customers. A well-designed store helps customers find the products they're looking for and encourages them to explore and make purchases.

By focusing on user experience, you can increase your store's conversion rate, leading to higher profits. Consider investing in professional web design or using e-commerce platforms with built-in design templates to optimize your store for conversion. If you want to see your e-commerce profits soar, it's time to optimize your store for conversion by implementing a user-friendly website design and smooth navigation. With ChatGPT's help, you'll create an e-commerce store that's both beautiful and functional, enticing customers to browse, explore, and ultimately make a purchase.

How about trying, "How can ChatGPT help me identify the most important elements of user-friendly website design and navigation for my e-commerce store to improve conversion rates?" or "What specific recommendations can ChatGPT provide for improving the user experience overall design of my e-commerce store to encourage more purchases?"

By tapping into ChatGPT's vast knowledge, you can gather insights on best practices for e-commerce design, discover the latest trends in user experience, and even receive personalized recommendations on fine-tuning your store's layout. Your e-commerce store will become a well-oiled conversion machine, enticing customers to spend more, and boosting your bottom line.

So, get ready to watch your conversion rates skyrocket as you harness the power of ChatGPT to create a seamless, enjoyable shopping experience that keeps customers coming back for more. After all, a happy customer is a loyal customer, a recipe for long-term success.

You can ask, "Can ChatGPT provide examples of successful e-commerce stores with user-friendly designs and easy navigation, along with an analysis of the features that contribute to their success?" or "How can I use ChatGPT to stay updated on the latest trends in e-commerce design and user experience, ensuring my store remains competitive and appealing to customers?"

Crafting compelling calls-to-action with ChatGPT's help

An effective call-to-action (CTA) can be the difference between a customer making a purchase or leaving your store empty-handed. ChatGPT can help you craft compelling CTAs that encourage customers to act, such as "Buy Now," "Add to Cart," or "Sign Up for Exclusive Offers."

By utilizing the AI's understanding of persuasive language and consumer psychology, you can create CTAs that resonate with your target audience and drive higher conversion rates, ultimately increasing your profits.

It's time to level up your e-commerce game with powerful calls-to-action (CTAs) that can make your conversion rates soar. With ChatGPT's help, you'll be crafting irresistible CTAs that will entice customers to act, whether it's clicking "Buy Now," adding an item to their cart, or signing up for exclusive offers.

Just ask ChatGPT, "How can ChatGPT help me understand the key elements of an effective call-to-action (CTA) for my e-commerce store to increase conversion rates?" or "What specific recommendations can ChatGPT provide for crafting compelling CTAs tailored to my target audience's preferences and behavior?"

Let ChatGPT be your secret weapon for creating persuasive CTAs based on consumer psychology and effective language. By incorporating these powerful, AI-generated CTAs into your e-commerce store, you'll see a significant increase in conversion rates, ultimately boosting your profits and bringing you closer to that lifestyle above others.

So, future tycoons, don't hesitate to harness the power of ChatGPT for crafting CTAs that will make your customers eager to engage with your store. You'll be well on your way to building a thriving e-commerce empire that leaves your competitors in dust.

You can try asking, "Can ChatGPT analyze my current CTAs and provide suggestions for improvement based on best practices and consumer psychology?" or "How can I use ChatGPT to stay updated on the latest trends and research in crafting persuasive CTAs, ensuring my e-commerce store remains competitive and appealing to customers?"

Monitoring and analyzing store performance for continuous improvement

To ensure the ongoing success of your e-commerce store, it's essential to monitor and analyze its performance regularly. By tracking key metrics such as conversion rates, average order value, and bounce rates, you can identify areas for improvement and make data-driven decisions to optimize your store.

ChatGPT can assist in analyzing store data, providing insights into user behavior, and suggesting changes that can enhance the shopping experience and boost your store's profitability. By continuously refining your e-commerce strategy, you can stay ahead of the competition and grow your profits.

You can easily ask, "How can ChatGPT help me monitor and analyze key performance metrics for my e-commerce store to identify areas for improvement?" or "What insights can ChatGPT provide regarding user behavior patterns to help me optimize the shopping experience and increase conversion rates?"

By leveraging ChatGPT, you can uncover insights into user behavior and identify opportunities for improvement in your store. Whether it's enhancing the user experience, fine-tuning product descriptions, or adjusting the layout, ChatGPT provides actionable recommendations that can boost your store's conversion rates and, ultimately, your profits. Don't let the competition outpace you. Keep your store fresh and relevant by constantly refining your e-commerce strategy with the help of ChatGPT. By staying ahead of the curve, you'll be well on your way to achieving that millionaire lifestyle.

Just ask ChatGPT, "How can ChatGPT help me monitor and analyze key performance metrics for my e-commerce store to identify areas for improvement?" or "What insights can ChatGPT provide regarding user behavior patterns to help me optimize the shopping experience increase conversion rates?"

And now, for a random, tech-geeky ending: Why was the computer cold at the office? It left its Windows open! Remember, a well-optimized e-commerce store is like a cozy office - with ChatGPT's help, you can keep your store's "windows" closed to the competition and stay comfortably ahead in the race to the top!

Promoting Your E-commerce Store and Products

Developing a comprehensive marketing strategy for your store

A well-rounded marketing strategy is essential for driving traffic to your e-commerce store and increasing sales. This includes utilizing various channels such as search engine optimization (SEO), social media, email marketing, and paid advertising to reach your target audience.

By identifying your ideal customer profile, you can tailor your marketing efforts to resonate with them and ultimately drive conversions. Investing time and resources in developing a comprehensive marketing strategy will help you generate more revenue and grow your e-commerce business. Ready to skyrocket your e-commerce business to millionaire heights? It's time to capitalize on ChatGPT's prowess in developing a comprehensive marketing strategy for your store. With AI by your side, your marketing game will be unstoppable, reaching your target audience and driving those sales through the roof.

You can ask, "How can ChatGPT help me develop a comprehensive marketing strategy tailored to my e-commerce store and target audience?" or "What insights and suggestions can ChatGPT provide for effectively utilizing various marketing channels, such as SEO, social media, email marketing, and paid advertising?"

ChatGPT can be your secret weapon in tailoring marketing campaigns across various channels, such as SEO, social media, email marketing, and paid advertising. By understanding your ideal customer profile, AI helps create highly targeted and persuasive content, making your marketing efforts resonate with your audience like never before.

Your e-commerce store's success doesn't stop at optimization and product presentation. Seamlessly blend your marketing strategy with ChatGPT's assistance to ensure a continuous flow of growth and conversions. It's time to unleash the full potential of AI-powered marketing and reach the pinnacle of e-commerce success.

Just ask, "Can ChatGPT assist me in creating highly targeted and persuasive content for my marketing campaigns based on my ideal customer profile?" or "How can I leverage ChatGPT's AI capabilities to continuously refine my e-commerce store's marketing strategy and stay ahead of the competition?"

Leveraging ChatGPT for social media

Time to dominate social media and drive your e-commerce sales to new heights! With ChatGPT by your side, crafting attention-grabbing posts and captions becomes a breeze. The AI-powered tool helps you connect with your audience and keeps them engaged, ensuring your store stays at the top of their minds.

ChatGPT is also a game-changer for your email marketing campaigns. It helps create personalized and irresistible emails encouraging recipients to visit your store and shop until they drop. Your open and click-through rates will soar as ChatGPT generates content that speaks directly to your audience's needs and desires. Paid advertising? No problem! ChatGPT, has you covered there, too, creating effective ad copy that captivates potential customers and entices them to click through to your store. Your return on investment will soar as you optimize your marketing efforts with the help of ChatGPT.

"How can ChatGPT assist me in creating engaging content for social media, email marketing campaigns, and paid advertising to drive traffic and increase sales for my e-commerce store?" or "What strategies and tactics can ChatGPT recommend to effectively leverage AI-generated content across various marketing channels for my e-commerce store?"

As we wrap up this exhilarating exploration of e-commerce and ChatGPT, let's add a random tech-geeky ending: What do you call a group of 8 hobbits? A hobbyte! So, gather your hobbyte of marketing strategies, and with ChatGPT's help, embark on the quest to e-commerce success and millionaire glory!

Building a strong brand presence

Ready to make a lasting impression on your customers? It's time to build a strong brand presence that fosters trust and loyalty. ChatGPT is here to make it happen, ensuring your messaging and visuals are consistent across your e-commerce store and marketing channels.

Now you have an AI-powered tool that helps you create a cohesive brand identity that resonates with your target audience. With ChatGPT, you can generate content that aligns with your brand's voice and style, providing a unified message across all touchpoints. The result? Increased customer loyalty, repeat purchases, and higher profits for your e-commerce store.

As you leverage ChatGPT to establish your brand's presence, your e-commerce store will stand out in the crowded market, bringing you closer to your financial dreams. It's time to embrace the power of AI to elevate your brand and propel your e-commerce store to success.

You can easily ask, "How can ChatGPT help me develop a strong brand presence and create a cohesive brand identity across all touchpoints for my e-commerce store?" or "What specific strategies can I use with ChatGPT to ensure my messaging and visuals are consistent, fostering trust and loyalty among my target audience?"

Chapter 7: Ghostwriting and Self-Publishing for Profit

Understanding Ghostwriting and Self-Publishing

Defining ghostwriting and its role in the writing industry

Ghostwriting is a practice in which a writer creates content for someone else who takes credit for the work. This is common in various industries, including books, articles, blogs, and speeches. Ghostwriters are often in high demand, as many individuals and businesses require well-written content but may lack the time or writing skills to create it themselves.

By working with ChatGPT, ghostwriters can leverage the power of AI to create high-quality content more efficiently, allowing them to take on more projects and increase their earnings. Welcome to the world of ghostwriting, where you can make a fortune by creating content for clients who take credit for your work. Ready to unlock the true potential of ghostwriting? With ChatGPT, you can take your writing game to the next level, increasing efficiency and elevating the quality of your content.

Ask ChatGPT, "How can ChatGPT help me improve my efficiency and content quality as a ghostwriter?" or "What are some strategies for using ChatGPT to take on more projects and maximize my earnings in the ghostwriting industry?"

As a ghostwriter aiming for millionaire status, you'll be thrilled that ChatGPT can be your secret weapon. With its AI capabilities, you can create top-notch content faster, allowing you to take on more projects and boost your earnings.

Think about it: the more efficiently you work, the more projects you can handle, and the higher your income becomes. By leveraging ChatGPT, you'll be one step closer to your millionaire dream, all while delivering outstanding content for your clients.

You can easily ask, "What are some examples of content types and industries where ChatGPT can assist me as a ghostwriter?" or "Who are the best experts to contact in the [your niche] niche to help me with ghostwriting opportunities?"

The benefits and challenges of self-publishing

Self-publishing allows writers to bypass traditional publishing houses and retain full control over their work, from content creation to marketing and distribution. This offers many benefits, such as higher royalty rates and creative freedom. However, self-publishing also presents challenges, including writers needing to handle all aspects of the publishing process themselves.

ChatGPT can be a valuable resource for self-publishing writers, as it can assist with content generation, editing, and even marketing materials. By utilizing ChatGPT's capabilities, writers can increase their productivity and income potential in self-publishing. If you're an ambitious writer who dreams of becoming a self-publishing millionaire, look no further! With ChatGPT, you have a powerful AI-driven tool to help you overcome the challenges of self-publishing and reach your financial goals.

Imagine having an AI assistant to help you write, edit, and create marketing materials for your self-published books! ChatGPT is that assistant, ready to help you increase productivity and income in self-publishing.

Just ask, "What are some specific ways ChatGPT can help me handle the publishing process when self-publishing my work?" or "How can I use ChatGPT to overcome common challenges ghostwriter authors face in contacting, marketing and distribution?"

No more struggling with writer's block or worrying about creating the perfect promotional materials. With ChatGPT, you can focus on what you do best, writing amazing content, while the AI handles the rest. The more you work together, the closer you'll reach your entrepreneurial dreams.

Just ask ChatGPT, "Can you provide examples of how ChatGPT can help me generate content, edit, and create marketing materials for my self-published books?" or "Outline the plot and acts for my bestselling fiction book about sci-fi and a cyborg hero who beats the bad guys with a plot twist included."

In conclusion, ChatGPT can be your secret weapon in your self-publishing journey, making the process smoother and more profitable. By leveraging AI's capabilities, you can take control of your writing career and achieve financial success.

Identifying your niche and target audience

To succeed in ghostwriting and self-publishing, it's crucial to identify a niche and target audience that aligns with your expertise and interests. This allows you to create content that resonates with readers and stands out in a competitive market. ChatGPT can be instrumental in helping you research and analyze different niches, as well as develop a deeper understanding of your target audience's needs and preferences.

Using AI to gain insights into your niche and audience, you can create more targeted and appealing content, ultimately leading to higher earnings in your ghostwriting or self-publishing endeavors. Unlock the door to your digital nomad dreams by mastering the art of identifying your niche and target audience in ghostwriting and self-publishing! ChatGPT is here to elevate your expertise and ensure you create content that resonates with readers in a competitive market. ChatGPT's AI-driven research capabilities will help you analyze different niches and gain insights into your target audience's needs and preferences. With this information, you can develop content that captivates your audience and sets you apart from the competition.

You can ask, "What are the key strategies I can use with ChatGPT to identify my niche and better understand my target audience in both ghostwriting and self-publishing?" or "How can ChatGPT specifically help me create more targeted and appealing content that resonates with my audience and leads to higher earnings in ghostwriting and self-publishing?"

In your pursuit of riches, remember that targeted and appealing content is the key to unlocking higher earnings in ghostwriting and self-publishing endeavors. With ChatGPT by your side, you'll be on the fast track to becoming a writing industry millionaire.

Developing Writing Skills with ChatGPT

Enhancing your writing skills for ghostwriting projects

To excel in ghostwriting, continually developing and refining your writing skills is essential. This involves staying current with industry trends, mastering various writing styles, and adapting your voice to suit your clients' needs. Working with ChatGPT can help you improve your writing skills by providing insights, suggestions, and inspiration.

By studying AI-generated content and implementing its techniques, you can broaden your writing capabilities and produce higher-quality content for your clients, leading to increased earnings. To excel in this lucrative field, it's essential to keep your skills sharp, adapt to different styles, and deliver content that meets your clients' expectations.

Try asking, "How can I use ChatGPT to help me stay current with industry trends and master various writing styles for my ghostwriting projects?" or "What specific techniques and insights can I learn from AI-generated content to improve my writing skills and better adapt my voice to suit my clients' needs?"

ChatGPT is here to be your writing assistant, guiding you as you develop and refine your skills. By studying AI-generated content, you'll gain insights, suggestions, and inspiration that will help you elevate your writing game. As you grow your abilities and produce higher-quality content, your clients will be ecstatic, leading to increased earnings and a sterling reputation in the ghostwriting world. Remember, in ghostwriting, your skills are the golden ticket to success!

You can ask, "How can I use ChatGPT to help me stay current with industry trends and master various writing styles for my ghostwriting projects?" or "What are some key search terms you can generate for my content to improve my writing skills and better adapt my style to suit my client's needs?"

So, buckle up and embrace the journey to becoming a top performing ghostwriter with ChatGPT as your co-pilot. And for a funny ending, why do AI writers never get tired? Because they have endless "byte-sized" energy! Keep laughing, keep learning, and keep earning with ChatGPT by your side!

Leveraging ChatGPT to generate ideas, outlines, and drafts

One of the challenges all ghostwriters face is generating fresh ideas and crafting engaging content for various clients. ChatGPT can be a valuable partner in this process, helping you brainstorm ideas, create outlines, and even produce initial drafts for your projects.

Using AI's ability to analyze large amounts of data and generate unique insights, you can streamline your creative process and ensure your content is original and engaging. This saves time and allows you to take on more projects and increase your income as a ghostwriter.

When you're on the road to becoming a millionaire ghostwriter, leveraging ChatGPT to generate ideas, outlines, and drafts is a surefire way to accelerate your success! Say goodbye to writer's block and hello to a wealth of creativity and productivity.

To help ask, "How can I use ChatGPT to effectively brainstorm ideas and create outlines for my ghostwriting projects?" or "What are some tips for utilizing ChatGPT's data analysis capabilities to generate unique insights and produce engaging content for my clients?"

With ChatGPT's impressive data analysis capabilities, you can uncover unique insights and craft original, engaging content that your clients will adore. The more you utilize this powerful AI tool, the more you'll be able to maximize your time, allowing you to take on additional projects and boost your income!

Try asking, "How can I maximize my time and increase my income by using ChatGPT to streamline my creative process in ghostwriting?" or "What strategies can I use to take full advantage of ChatGPT's capabilities to boost my productivity and reach my financial goals in ghostwriting?"

By embracing ChatGPT as your ghostwriting ally, you'll be well on your way to achieving that millionaire business owner status. So, let's keep up the momentum, and remember: the sky's the limit when you have AI on your side!

Editing and proofreading your work with AI assistance

Maintaining high-quality standards is crucial for success in ghostwriting. This involves creating engaging content and ensuring that your work is free from errors and inconsistencies. ChatGPT can assist you in the editing and proofreading process by identifying grammar and punctuation issues, suggesting improvements in sentence structure, and offering alternative phrasing to enhance readability.

Using AI to streamline your editing process, you can deliver polished content to your clients faster, ultimately boosting your reputation and earning potential in the ghostwriting field.

Ask, "How can I effectively use ChatGPT to edit and proofread my ghostwriting projects for grammar, punctuation, and sentence structure improvements?" or "What are some techniques to optimize my editing process using AI assistance and enhance the readability of my work?"

Transform your ghostwriting career into a money-making machine by leveraging ChatGPT for editing and proofreading. High-quality content is the key to unlocking millionaire status, and ChatGPT can help you achieve that polished, error-free writing that clients love. Save time and energy by using AI to identify grammar and punctuation issues, improve sentence structure, and enhance readability. With ChatGPT's assistance, you'll deliver top-notch content to your clients, fast!

Get a great answer with the prompt, "How can I leverage ChatGPT's editing capabilities to boost my reputation and earning potential as a ghostwriter?" or "What strategies can I employ to ensure that my work is polished and error-free using AI assistance, leading to higher-paying projects and increased income?"

Streamlining your editing process will boost your reputation as a ghostwriter, unlocking the door to higher-paying projects and a more prosperous future. Embrace the power of AI and watch your income skyrocket!

Finding and Managing Ghostwriting Projects

Sourcing ghostwriting projects and establishing client relationships

Finding and securing ghostwriting projects is crucial for generating income in this field. To source potential clients, consider networking within your niche, joining online platforms and communities dedicated to freelance writing, and marketing your services through a professional website and social media channels.

By showcasing your expertise, writing samples, and testimonials, you can attract clients and begin You can attract clients and begin building lasting relationships by showcasing your expertise, writing samples, and testimonials, increasing your chances of landing lucrative ghostwriting opportunities. Multiply your income as a ghostwriter by mastering the art of finding and managing projects. Embrace the power of networking within your niche, tap into online freelance writing communities, and showcase your prowess with a professional website and social media presence. The more you put yourself out there, the more opportunities you'll attract!

You can quickly ask, "What are some effective strategies for networking and marketing my ghostwriting services to potential clients within my niche?" or "How can I use ChatGPT to create captivating marketing materials that showcase my skills and attract clients?"

ChatGPT can be your secret weapon in creating compelling marketing materials that showcase your skills and reel in clients. Let AI do the heavy lifting while you focus on building strong relationships and delivering exceptional work.

As you manage multiple ghostwriting projects, ChatGPT can also help you stay organized and efficient, allowing you to maximize your productivity and income potential. The road to wealth status starts with taking advantage of the tools at your disposal, and ChatGPT is one tool that can truly make a difference.

Just ask, "How can I leverage ChatGPT to manage multiple ghostwriting projects more efficiently and stay organized?" or "What are some specific ways ChatGPT can help me maximize my productivity and income potential as a ghostwriter?"

Now, for a random tech geeky ending: Just like the famous Moore's Law states that the number of transistors on a microchip double approximately every two years, you too can double your ghostwriting success by harnessing the power of AI with ChatGPT! So, go forth and conquer the world of ghostwriting with technology by your side!

Negotiating contracts, timelines, and payment terms

Once you've secured a ghostwriting project, it's essential to negotiate contracts, timelines, and payment terms with your clients. Clearly outline the project's scope, expected deliverables, deadlines, and payment structure to avoid misunderstandings and ensure a smooth working relationship.

ChatGPT can help you draft professional contracts and communicate effectively with clients, making the negotiation process more efficient and potentially increasing your earnings by helping you secure favorable terms.

Become a pro at negotiating your ghostwriting projects' contracts, timelines, and payment terms. By clearly outlining the project scope, deliverables, deadlines, and payment structures, you can prevent misunderstandings and ensure a smooth, productive working relationship with clients.

You can ask, "What are some key elements to include in a ghostwriting contract to ensure clarity and protect my interests?" or "How can I use ChatGPT to draft professional contracts and effectively communicate during negotiations?"

ChatGPT can be a game changer in drafting professional contracts and communicating effectively during negotiations. By tapping into the power of AI, you can make the negotiation process more efficient, enabling you to secure favorable terms and ultimately increase your earnings as a ghostwriter. By blending AI technology with your negotiating prowess, you can achieve your above average dreams and make your mark in the competitive world of ghostwriting. The sky's the limit when you've got ChatGPT in your corner, helping you navigate the complexities of ghostwriting contracts and client communication.

Just ask ChatGPT, "What negotiation strategies can I use to secure favorable terms for my ghostwriting projects?" or "Based on these terms and conditions of the client, what would be the best ghostwriter output outline I need for each book chapter?"

Imagine yourself as a high-powered CPU, processing data and making lightning-speed decisions. With ChatGPT as your co-processor, you can amplify your performance and turbocharge your ghostwriting success. Together, you'll be an unstoppable force, crushing negotiations and paving the way to fortune!

Meeting client expectations and maintaining professionalism

As an artificial intelligence powered ghostwriter, your success depends on your ability to meet or exceed client expectations consistently. This involves delivering high-quality content on time, maintaining clear communication, and being receptive to feedback. ChatGPT can help you manage your projects more efficiently by offering content generation, editing, and proofreading support, ensuring your work aligns with your client's requirements.

Maintaining professionalism and utilizing AI assistance can build a strong reputation in the ghostwriting industry, leading to more projects and increased income. Meeting client expectations and maintaining professionalism are critical to your ghostwriting success. You can set yourself apart from the competition by delivering top-quality content on time, keeping communication lines open, and being receptive to feedback. But how can you do all this and still have time to grow your business? The answer: ChatGPT!

For great answers, you can ask, "How can I use ChatGPT to ensure my work consistently meets or exceeds client expectations in ghostwriting projects?" or "What strategies can I implement to maintain clear communication and professionalism with my clients, with the help of ChatGPT?"

This powerful AI tool can revolutionize the way you manage your ghostwriting projects. With ChatGPT's content generation, editing, and proofreading support, you can ensure your work perfectly aligns with your client's requirements. You'll impress clients with your efficiency and build a strong reputation in the industry, ultimately leading to a steady stream of projects and a skyrocketing income.

You can ask, "In what ways can ChatGPT specifically help me manage multiple ghostwriting projects while maintaining high-quality standards and meeting deadlines?" or "How can I leverage ChatGPT's capabilities to improve my workflow, productivity, and overall client satisfaction in the ghostwriting industry?"

By combining your professionalism with ChatGPT's capabilities, you can make your mark as a millionaire ghostwriter in no time. Watch your earnings soar as you consistently meet and exceed client expectations while leveraging AI assistance to enhance your workflow and productivity.

Self-Publishing Your eBooks

Selecting the right self-publishing platform

Choosing the right self-publishing platform is crucial for maximizing your eBook's visibility and profit potential. Factors to consider when selecting a platform include the control you retain over pricing, royalties, and distribution and the available marketing tools and resources. Popular platforms like Amazon Kindle Direct Publishing (KDP) and Draft2Digital, offer various benefits and features to suit different needs.

ChatGPT can help you research and compare platforms, making choosing the best option for your eBook easier and increasing your chances of success.

When self-publishing your eBooks, choosing the right platform is the key to unlocking massive visibility and profits. You want to ensure you control pricing, royalties, distribution, and access to effective marketing tools and resources. There's much to consider with platforms like Amazon KDP and Draft2Digital.

You can ask ChatGPT, "How can ChatGPT assist me in researching and comparing self-publishing platforms to maximize my eBook's visibility and profit potential?" or "What are the specific benefits and features of Amazon KDP, Draft2Digital and Publish Drive, that I should consider when choosing a self-publishing platform?"

This versatile AI tool can help you research and compare platforms, making the decision process a breeze. Instead of spending hours digging through information, let ChatGPT do the heavy lifting and give you a clear picture of your options. This will save you time and ensure you're making the best decision for your eBook. I will give you a recommendation beside the AI that personally I use Draft2Digital, which combined companies with Smashing Words, for their ease of global reach. But you will find out the other options available to you with the help of ChatGPT.

With ChatGPT's assistance, you can zero in on the ideal platform for your eBook, setting the stage for increased visibility, sales, and, ultimately, higher earnings. You'll be on your way to one of the most recognized in the industry as you capitalize on the perfect self-publishing platform, bringing your eBook to readers worldwide who are eager to dive into your content.

A Great prompt to use is, "How can I leverage ChatGPT's capabilities to save time and make informed decisions when selecting a self-publishing platform for my eBook?" or "What strategies can I use, with the help of ChatGPT, to capitalize on the perfect self-publishing platform and maximize my eBook's sales and earnings?"

As you revel in your growing success, picture yourself and ChatGPT as a futuristic duo – an author and AI working in perfect harmony to navigate the self-publishing landscape. Together, you'll create a self-publishing empire where your eBooks dominate the market and your profits soar. Buckle up because, with ChatGPT by your side, it will be a thrilling ride!

Formatting and designing your eBook for optimal reader experience

To ensure your self-published eBook is well-received, it's essential to focus on formatting and design for a seamless reader experience. This includes organizing content in a logical manner, using consistent formatting styles, and incorporating visuals when appropriate.

ChatGPT can assist you in generating well-structured content, proofreading, and providing suggestions for layout and design elements. By optimizing your eBook's presentation, you can create a more engaging and professional product, ultimately driving more sales and revenue.

When it comes to self-publishing, creating a visually appealing and easy-to-read eBook is crucial for capturing readers' attention and increasing sales. Formatting and design play a significant role in delivering an optimal reader experience. This is where ChatGPT comes in – your ultimate secret weapon in generating well-structured content, proofreading, and suggesting layout and design elements.

You can ask, "How can ChatGPT help me create well-structured content and ensure my eBook's formatting and design are optimized for a seamless reader experience?" or "What specific layout and design elements should I consider incorporating into my eBook to make it more engaging and professional?"

With ChatGPT's assistance, you can create a professional-looking eBook that not only engages your readers but also keeps them coming back for more. Imagine your eBook standing out among the competition with its impeccable design and layout, compelling potential buyers to click "purchase" without hesitation. The more captivating your eBook is, the more sales you'll generate.

ChatGPT's capabilities continue beyond content generation and proofreading. The AI tool can also help you research the latest design trends and best practices, ensuring your eBook is visually appealing and up to date. As you implement ChatGPT's suggestions, you'll witness your eBook transform into a masterpiece that resonates with your target audience, driving more sales and skyrocketing your revenue.

Ask ChatGPT, "How can ChatGPT help me create well-structured content and ensure my eBook's formatting and design are like one of the top 100 on Amazon?" or "What specific layout and design elements should I consider incorporating into my eBook to make it more engaging and professional?"

With ChatGPT by your side, you'll conquer the self-publishing world, one beautifully formatted and designed eBook at a time. As your sales increase and your reputation grows, you'll find yourself closer to that lifestyle you've always dreamed of. So, gear up for an incredible journey into the realm of self-publishing, where ChatGPT will be your co-pilot, helping you achieve the success you deserve!

Creating a book cover and metadata to attract readers

An eye-catching book cover and well-crafted metadata play a significant role in attracting readers to your self-published eBook. The cover should visually communicate the book's genre and tone, while the metadata, including the title, description, and keywords, should be optimized for searchability and discoverability.

ChatGPT can help you brainstorm ideas for book covers and create compelling metadata that appeals to your target audience, increasing the likelihood of your eBook being found and purchased by potential readers. Investing time and effort in these critical elements can boost your eBook's visibility and profitability.

If you're aiming to become a self-publishing millionaire, never underestimate the power of an alluring book cover and well-crafted metadata. These elements can make or break your eBook's success, luring readers to explore your masterpiece or leaving it undiscovered in the vast ocean of self-published works.

You can quickly ask, "How can ChatGPT help me brainstorm ideas for an eye-catching book cover that effectively communicates my eBook's genre and tone?" or "What are some tips for creating compelling metadata, including title, description, and keywords, to optimize my eBook's searchability and discoverability?"

ChatGPT is your secret weapon to create captivating book covers and metadata that resonate with your target audience. The AI can help you brainstorm ideas for book covers, guiding you to design a cover that captures the essence of your book and entices readers to click on your title. With ChatGPT's assistance, your book cover will stand out as a magnet for potential readers.

But that's not all! ChatGPT also empowers you to optimize your eBook's metadata, including the title, description, and keywords. Using AI-generated suggestions, you can craft metadata that maximizes searchability and discoverability, ensuring your book reaches the right audience. The more visible your eBook becomes, the higher the chances of generating sales and boosting your profits.

An amazing prompt to use is, "Can ChatGPT provide examples of effective book covers and metadata in my specific genre to help me understand what works best for my target audience?" or "What strategies can I use, with the help of ChatGPT, to ensure my book cover and metadata stand out among the competition and attract more potential readers to my eBook?"

By combining the power of ChatGPT with your dedication to creating the perfect book cover and metadata, you'll witness your eBook sales skyrocket, propelling you towards the business empire you've always felt you deserved. So, buckle up and get ready to dominate the self-publishing world, one stunning book cover and well-optimized metadata at a time. With ChatGPT by your side, there's no stopping you from reaching the pinnacle of success in the self-publishing arena!

Marketing and Monetizing

Developing a book marketing strategy with ChatGPT's support

A well-planned book marketing strategy is essential for driving sales and generating profit from your self-published books. With ChatGPT's support, you can develop a comprehensive marketing plan that includes identifying your target audience, conducting market research, and creating promotional materials.

ChatGPT can also help you craft persuasive sales copy, social media content, and email campaigns to effectively promote your book. By utilizing AI assistance in developing and implementing your marketing strategy, you can increase your book's reach and revenue potential. To become a self-publishing millionaire, your book marketing strategy must be top-notch. Fret not, because ChatGPT is here to propel your marketing efforts to new heights, ensuring your self-published books get the attention they deserve.

You can ask, "How can ChatGPT help me develop a comprehensive marketing plan for my self-published book, including identifying my target audience and conducting market research?" or "What are some examples of promotional materials that ChatGPT can help me create to effectively market my book?"

Harness the power of ChatGPT to identify your target audience with laser-like precision. With AI-generated insights, you can conduct thorough market research to understand your readers' preferences and create tailor-made promotional materials that resonate with them. Your marketing plan will be fine-tuned, giving you an edge in the competitive world of self-publishing.

ChatGPT is your trusty companion in crafting persuasive sales copy, attention-grabbing social media content, and engaging email campaigns that showcase your book's unique selling points. With the AI's assistance, you'll be able to effectively communicate the value of your book, driving more sales and skyrocketing your revenue.

Ask ChatGPT, "Can ChatGPT provide tips and examples for crafting persuasive sales copy, engaging social media content, and email campaigns that will resonate with my target audience?" or "How can I use ChatGPT to track the success of my marketing efforts and continually optimize my strategy for maximum reach and revenue potential?"

Get ready to embrace the full potential of ChatGPT as it supercharges your marketing strategy, turning your self-published eBooks into profitable powerhouses. As your book's reach expands, you'll be well on your way to achieving that millionaire milestone you've always aspired to. And now, as you embark on this thrilling journey, remember to keep your eyes on the prize and your marketing game strong with ChatGPT's unmatched support!

Building an online presence and Engaging with Readers

Building a strong online presence is vital for self-published authors to connect with readers and generate buzz around their books. Establishing a website, author blog, and social media profiles can help you showcase your work, share updates, and engage with your audience.

ChatGPT can assist you in creating engaging content for these platforms and managing and responding to reader comments and messages. By maintaining an active online presence and fostering genuine connections with your readers, you can increase your book's visibility, attract new readers, and boost sales. Building a robust online presence is the key to unlocking your book's full sales potential in your quest to become a self-publishing millionaire. ChatGPT is the secret ingredient that can help you cultivate a thriving online community around your work and keep readers coming back for more.

You can ask, "How can ChatGPT help me create engaging content for my website, author blog, and social media profiles to build a strong online presence and connect with readers?" or "What are some examples of content types and topics that ChatGPT can generate to help me showcase my work and engage with my audience?"

With ChatGPT by your side, your website, author blog, and social media profiles will be brimming with engaging, high-quality content tailored to your target audience. Share updates, behind-the-scenes insights, and more with the help of ChatGPT's content creation abilities, crafting compelling narratives that keep your readers hooked.

But that's not all! ChatGPT can also help you manage and respond to reader comments and messages, ensuring that you're fostering genuine connections with your audience. Engaging with your readers is a powerful way to build loyalty, attract new fans, and drive more book sales.

As you build your online empire, you'll find that ChatGPT is an invaluable ally in creating a magnetic presence that propels your self-publishing business to unparalleled heights. Keep pushing the boundaries of what's possible, and before you know it, you'll be the self-publishing millionaire you've always thought that would be nice, but... Well, no more. Consider it guaranteed.

Another great prompt to use is "Can ChatGPT provide guidance on managing and responding to reader comments and messages to foster genuine connections and increase reader loyalty?" or "How can I use ChatGPT to continually optimize my online presence and content strategy to maximize visibility, attract new readers, and boost sales?"

And now, as you embark on this exhilarating journey to dominate the world of self-publishing, always remember to keep your online presence strong, your content game on point, and your connections genuine. With ChatGPT in your corner, there's no limit to what you can achieve. So, buckle up and enjoy the ride because the sky's the limit!

Exploring additional revenue streams

To maximize the profit potential of your self-published books, consider exploring additional revenue streams such as audiobooks and translations. The growing popularity of audiobooks offers a significant opportunity to reach a broader audience, and translating your book into other languages can help you tap into global markets.

ChatGPT can assist you in researching potential markets, finding suitable narrators or translators, and creating promotional materials for these new formats. By diversifying your revenue streams, you can increase your book's earning potential and establish yourself as a successful self-published author.

Ready to skyrocket your self-publishing income and join the millionaire's club? Embracing additional revenue streams like audiobooks and translations is a game-changing strategy that can take your earnings to the next level. With ChatGPT by your side, conquering these new frontiers has never been easier.

An amazing prompt to use is, "How can ChatGPT help me research potential markets and opportunities for audiobooks and translations to diversify my revenue streams?" or "What are some strategies ChatGPT can suggest to successfully promote and market my self-published books in new formats, such as audiobooks and translations?"

The booming audiobook market is a goldmine waiting to be tapped, and ChatGPT can support you in researching the best opportunities to suit your genre and target audience. Find the perfect narrator to bring your words to life and create a compelling listening experience that will have readers coming back for more.

But why stop there? Translating your book into other languages unlocks the door to global markets, vastly expanding your potential readership. ChatGPT can help you identify the most lucrative language markets and find skilled translators to ensure your book's message resonates with readers worldwide.

With ChatGPT's assistance, you can also craft promotional materials tailored to these new formats, capturing audiences' attention far and wide. By diversifying your revenue streams, you'll boost your book's earning potential and solidify your status as a self-publishing powerhouse.

You can ask, "Can ChatGPT guide finding suitable narrators or translators for my self-published books and evaluate their skills or compatibility with my content?" or "How can I use ChatGPT to create promotional materials tailored to audiobooks and translations, ensuring I effectively reach new audiences and boost my book's earning potential?"

So, what are you waiting for? It's time to embrace the thrill of exploring new markets, formats, and opportunities. With ChatGPT as your trusty co-pilot, the world is your oyster, and there's no telling just how high your self-publishing empire can soar. Onward and upward, fellow literary entrepreneur!

Chapter 8: AI-Assisted Copywriting and Marketing

The Power of AI in Copywriting and Marketing

The Role of AI in Modern Copywriting and marketing efforts

Embrace the future of copywriting and marketing with AI-driven tools like ChatGPT, and watch as your business soars to new heights of success. By leveraging the unmatched capabilities of AI, you'll create captivating content that resonates with your audience and delivers astonishing results.

The secret to AI's prowess in copywriting and marketing lies in its ability to generate high-quality, persuasive, and engaging content that drives conversions and boosts revenue. ChatGPT can produce compelling copy for various marketing channels, including websites, email campaigns, and social media. With AI at the helm, you'll save time and effort, allowing you to focus on other aspects of your business.

Just use the prompt to help you, "How can I use ChatGPT to create captivating content for various marketing channels, such as websites, email campaigns, and social media?" or "What are some examples of persuasive and engaging headlines that ChatGPT can generate to help drive conversions and boost revenue?"

But the benefits don't end there! AI can also provide powerful insights and analytics to guide your marketing strategy. From identifying trending topics to understanding audience preferences, ChatGPT's data-driven approach will help you make informed decisions that maximize the effectiveness of your marketing efforts.

By incorporating AI into your copywriting and marketing endeavors, you're positioning yourself at the cutting edge of your industry. As competition intensifies, those who harness the power of AI will have a significant advantage, attracting customers with their irresistible content and accelerating their journey toward a seven-figure fortune.

How about asking, "How can ChatGPT provide insights and analytics to guide my marketing strategy, identify trending topics such as car stereos, and understand audience preferences?" or "What are some tips for effectively incorporating AI into my copywriting and marketing efforts to stay ahead of the competition and accelerate my journey toward becoming a millionaire?"

So, buckle up, and let ChatGPT turbocharge your copywriting and marketing efforts. With the extraordinary power of AI at your fingertips, there's no limit to the success you can achieve. And remember, as you ascend the ladder to stardom, AI's helping you reach new heights, one exceptional piece of content at a time.

What are the benefits of using ChatGPT for copywriting and marketing tasks?

Ready to transform your copywriting and marketing game and reap the rewards? Look no further than ChatGPT, the AI-driven powerhouse that's taking the world of content creation by storm. With ChatGPT in your arsenal, you're poised to skyrocket your profits, leaving your competitors in dust.

The time-saving benefits of ChatGPT cannot be overstated. Forget spending hours agonizing over the perfect headline or email subject line – ChatGPT can generate eye-catching, persuasive copy in seconds. This means you can produce more content faster, allowing you to focus on other critical aspects of your business.

You can ask, "What are some examples of how ChatGPT can generate eye-catching, subtle yet powerful copy for headlines, email subject lines, and other marketing materials?" or "How can I use ChatGPT to produce more content faster and streamline my copywriting and marketing efforts?"

But the advantages don't stop there. ChatGPT's ability to create personalized and targeted content will make your audience feel understood and valued, driving engagement and conversions. You'll see increased sales by delivering tailored messaging that resonates with your audience, and your millionaire dreams will inch closer to reality. And let's not forget about data. ChatGPT's sophisticated analytics capabilities will help you uncover hidden trends and make data-driven decisions that propel your marketing strategy forward. By understanding what works and what doesn't, you can optimize your campaigns, boost your ROI, and grow your income at an unprecedented rate.

Just ask ChatGPT, "How can ChatGPT help me create personalized and targeted content that drives engagement and conversions for my audience?" or "What are some specific ways ChatGPT's sophisticated analytics capabilities can help me uncover hidden trends and make data-driven decisions to optimize my marketing campaigns?"

In a world where standing out from the crowd is the key to success, ChatGPT is the tool that will elevate your copywriting and marketing efforts to new heights. So, gear up because, with ChatGPT in your corner, you're about to embark on a thrilling journey toward unparalleled prosperity.

Key considerations for implementing AI in your marketing strategy

When integrating AI, like ChatGPT, into your marketing strategy, it's essential to consider several factors to maximize its potential. First, ensure that the AI-generated content aligns with your brand voice and messaging. Next, be mindful of the ethical implications of using AI-generated content, and always maintain transparency with your audience.

Finally, continually monitor and evaluate the performance of your AI-assisted marketing efforts to optimize your strategies and drive better results. By thoughtfully incorporating ChatGPT into your marketing plan, you can enhance your campaigns, increase conversions, and generate more income. Are you ready to take your marketing strategy to the next level and watch your profits soar? Implementing ChatGPT into your marketing plan is the game-changer you've been searching for. By carefully considering key factors during integration, you'll harness the full potential of AI, and spend less time worrying about how to achieve your goals.

You can ask with a great prompt such as, "How can I ensure that the AI-generated content produced by ChatGPT aligns with my brand voice and messaging?" or "What are some ethical implications of using AI-generated content and how can I maintain transparency with my audience?"

Consistency is crucial when it comes to brand voice and messaging. With ChatGPT, you can ensure that every piece of AI-generated content aligns with your unique brand identity. This consistency will strengthen your brand and make your message resonate with your audience, boosting engagement and driving sales.

Ethics and transparency are vital when using AI-generated content. Be upfront with your audience about your use of AI – it's the responsible thing to do, and your audience will appreciate your honesty. Besides, they'll be amazed by the cutting-edge technology you're leveraging to deliver exceptional content tailored just for them. To truly capitalize on ChatGPT's capabilities, continuous monitoring and evaluation are essential. By analyzing the performance of your AI-driven marketing efforts, you can refine your strategies and identify new opportunities for growth. This constant optimization will increase conversion rates and significantly boost your bottom line.

Just ask, "How can ChatGPT help me create consistent content that strengthens my brand and resonates with my target audience?" or "What are some best practices for monitoring and evaluating the performance of my AI-assisted marketing efforts to optimize strategies and drive better results?"

So, what are you waiting for? By integrating ChatGPT into your marketing strategy thoughtfully, you're unlocking a treasure trove of profit-generating potential. With the wind of AI-powered innovation at your back, you'll sail effortlessly toward the millionaire horizon. And as you journey onward, don't forget to give a nod to ChatGPT, the unsung hero propelling you to new heights of success. After all, even the most cutting-edge AI loves a little recognition now and then.

Crafting Persuasive Copy with ChatGPT

Developing compelling headlines and taglines with ChatGPT

Captivating headlines and taglines are crucial for grabbing your audience's attention and encouraging them to explore your content further. ChatGPT can be an asset in creating these essential elements, as it can quickly generate numerous options for you to choose from or refine.

By using AI-generated headlines and taglines that resonate with your target audience, you can increase click-through rates and drive more traffic to your content, ultimately leading to higher conversion rates and more income.

Unlock the secret to attention-grabbing headlines and taglines with the power of ChatGPT. When it comes to driving traffic and generating income, compelling headlines and taglines are your secret weapons. They draw your audience in, piquing their interest and persuading them to dive deeper into your content.

This is a great prompt: "How can I use ChatGPT to generate various attention-grabbing headlines and taglines for my marketing campaigns?" or "What are some tips for choosing the most effective AI-generated headlines and taglines that will resonate with my target audience?"

ChatGPT is the ace up your sleeve in the world of headline creation. By generating multiple headline and tagline options, you'll have a wealth of possibilities at your fingertips. This AI-driven approach means you'll have ample choices to refine and perfect your messaging, ensuring that your headlines hit the mark every time.

The impact of persuasive headlines and taglines on your bottom line cannot be overstated. With increased click-through rates and more traffic flowing to your content, you'll experience higher conversion rates, directly into more income. The millionaire life you've always dreamed of is just around the corner, and ChatGPT is the key to unlocking it.

Just ask, "How can I refine and perfect the AI-generated headlines and taglines provided by ChatGPT to ensure maximum impact on my target audience?" or "What are some examples of successful headlines and taglines generated by ChatGPT, and how can I apply their principles to my marketing efforts?"

As you rake in the profits and build your empire, remember that ChatGPT is the secret ingredient that supercharges your marketing efforts. And who knows? Perhaps one day, when the tale of your meteoric rise is told, ChatGPT will receive an honorary mention as the AI that helped spark your journey to the top. So, here's to you, the visionary entrepreneur, and your trusty sidekick ChatGPT – a dynamic duo ready to conquer the world, one headline at a time.

Writing engaging product descriptions and sales copy with ChatGPT

An essential aspect of effective marketing is creating persuasive and informative product descriptions and sales copies. ChatGPT can help you craft compelling content that highlights your product's unique features and benefits, appealing to your target audience's needs and desires.

By leveraging AI-generated content, you can create more engaging and persuasive copy that converts prospects into customers, ultimately increasing your revenue. Additionally, ChatGPT can help you maintain consistency across all marketing materials, ensuring a cohesive brand image that fosters trust and credibility with your audience. When it comes to skyrocketing your income, look no further than ChatGPT to create tantalizing product descriptions and irresistible sales copy that drives conversions. Unleash the full potential of AI-generated content to showcase your product's most enticing features and benefits, and watch as your target audience is drawn in like moths to a flame.

Just ask, "How can ChatGPT revolutionize my marketing strategy and help me craft compelling product descriptions and sales copy that convert prospects into loyal customers?" Or "In what ways can I unleash the full potential of AI-generated marketing content with ChatGPT to create engaging and persuasive product descriptions that increase my income?"

With ChatGPT at the helm, you'll be churning out engaging and persuasive content that turns prospects into loyal customers, fueling your journey to millionaire status. Consistency is king in the marketing world, and ChatGPT ensures a cohesive brand image that instils trust and credibility in your audience, paving the way for even more sales and revenue.

Imagine the possibilities: a steady stream of captivating content that showcases your products in the best light but also speaks directly to the heart of your customer's desires. This is the power of ChatGPT, and it's the key to unlocking a world of profits just waiting to be claimed.

As you watch your bank account grow and the world recognizes your success, you'll reflect on your decision to harness the power of ChatGPT with a sense of pride and satisfaction.

Personalizing content for different audience segments with ChatGPT

Personalized content is a powerful marketing tool; it speaks directly to individual audience segments and addresses their needs and preferences. ChatGPT can assist you in tailoring your copy to different audience segments by generating unique and targeted content variations, making your marketing efforts more effective.

By leveraging AI-generated personalized content, you can better connect with your audience, improve customer satisfaction, and increase conversion rates. As a result, this targeted approach to content creation can significantly contribute to generating more income from your marketing efforts. Picture this: you're a millionaire, all thanks to your ability to harness the power of personalized content with ChatGPT. This AI-driven tool is your secret weapon for creating copy that resonates with different audience segments, addressing their unique needs and preferences like never before. The future of marketing is here, and it's all about making deep connections with your target audience.

Just ask, "How can I use ChatGPT to generate engaging and persuasive product descriptions that showcase my fitness product's unique features and benefits?" or "What are some tips for creating AI-generated sales copy that connects with my target audience and drives conversions?"

By tapping into ChatGPT's potential for generating personalized content, you'll forge stronger bonds with your audience and see your conversion rates soar. With your marketing efforts fine-tuned to meet the specific desires of each audience segment, you'll be well on your way to amassing a fortune.

The key to unlocking this wealth lies in integrating ChatGPT seamlessly into your marketing strategy, turning it into a powerhouse for generating content that captivates and converts. Your competitors will be left in the dust, wondering how you connected with your audience on such a personal level. Even if they use ChatGPT they will be unlikely to have the advanced prompts available in this book, and the resources you have.

As you watch your income grow and your millionaire dreams become a reality, don't forget to acknowledge the role ChatGPT played in your success. Personalized content is the future of marketing, and with ChatGPT by your side, you're well-positioned to ride the wave of prosperity.

Try asking: "How can I ensure consistency in tone, style, and messaging across all AI-generated marketing materials, including product descriptions and sales copy?" or "What are some examples of successful product descriptions and sales copy generated by ChatGPT, and how can I apply their principles to my marketing efforts?"

So, as you prepare to embark on this exciting journey, remember that the perfect blend of creativity, technology, and marketing acumen is your ticket to a life of luxury. With ChatGPT in your corner, the sky's the limit – or maybe even the stars, as you shoot for the moon on your way to becoming a millionaire marketing mastermind.

Enhancing Email Marketing with ChatGPT

Creating attention-grabbing subject lines with ChatGPT

In email marketing, the subject line is often the first impression you make on your recipients. It can determine whether they open your email or send it straight to the trash. ChatGPT can help you craft eye-catching subject lines that pique your audience's curiosity and entice them to explore your message further.

By leveraging AI-generated subject lines, you can improve your email open rates, leading to increased engagement with your content, higher click-through rates, and, ultimately, more conversions and income.

Unlock the secret to becoming a millionaire with ChatGPT's ability to create attention-grabbing subject lines. Say goodbye to lackluster open rates and watch your email marketing efforts become a driving force behind your skyrocketing income. With ChatGPT's AI-generated subject lines, your audience won't be able to resist clicking on your emails, eager to discover the valuable content inside.

You can ask, "How can I use ChatGPT to generate attention-grabbing email subject lines that improve open rates and engagement?" or "What are some examples of successful AI-generated subject lines for various industries, and how can I apply their principles to my email marketing efforts?"

Imagine the power of having an AI-driven tool that churns out irresistible subject lines, compelling recipients to engage with your content. Your click-through rates will surge, and before you know it, you'll easily convert prospects into paying customers. ChatGPT is the missing piece in your email marketing strategy that can transform your business into a money-making machine.

The key to unleashing your millionaire potential lies in harnessing ChatGPT's power to create subject lines that resonate with your audience. Combining your marketing know-how with this advanced technology will create a winning formula that leads to an avalanche of income.

Try asking a quality prompt such as, "What strategies can I use to optimize my AI-generated subject lines for maximum impact and increased conversions in the financial industry?" or "How can I analyze the performance of my ChatGPT-generated subject lines to make data-driven improvements to my email marketing campaigns?"

So, as you prepare to dominate the email marketing landscape, remember that ChatGPT is your secret weapon. With its ability to craft captivating subject lines, your audience cannot resist your enticing emails, fueling your journey toward unimaginable wealth and success. And as you bask in the glow of your accomplishments, you'll wonder how you ever managed without ChatGPT by your side.

Writing personalized and effective email content with ChatGPT

Personalization is key in email marketing, as it can significantly impact your audience's engagement and response to your campaigns. ChatGPT can assist you in creating tailored email content that addresses your recipients' specific needs and interests, making your emails more relevant and engaging.

Using AI-generated content, you can quickly develop personalized messages that resonate with your audience and encourage them to act. This personalized approach can result in higher conversion rates, stronger customer relationships, and increased revenue for your business. Achieving financial freedom is within your grasp, and personalizing your email content with ChatGPT is the golden ticket you've been waiting for. The AI-generated content can craft tailored email messages that captivate your audience, leaving them eager to act and ultimately increasing your conversions and revenue.

You can ask, "How can I use ChatGPT to create personalized email content that addresses my recipients' specific needs and interests?" or "What are some examples of AI-generated email content demonstrating effective personalization, and how can I apply these techniques to my campaigns?"

Imagine the impact of having perfectly crafted, customized emails at your fingertips. Your recipients will feel like you're speaking directly to them, increasing their likelihood of engaging with your offers and promotions. By harnessing the power of ChatGPT, you can create a personalized email marketing strategy that will propel you toward unparalleled success and wealth.

Don't settle for generic email campaigns that fade into the background. Embrace the potential of ChatGPT and watch your open rates, click-through rates, and conversions soar. As you forge stronger connections with your audience, your business will thrive, and your income will reach new heights.

You can use a prompt like, "What strategies can I use to optimize my AI-generated personalized email content for maximum engagement and conversions?" or "What are the top three platforms for sending mass email campaigns from, and how should I best configure them to send 500 emails a day?"

This will allow you a flexible approach to mass email marketing but remember that ChatGPT is the ultimate game-changer for your email marketing campaigns. With its incredible ability to create personalized content, your audience will be enticed and engaged like never before. And as your conversions and income climb, you'll look back on the day you embraced ChatGPT as the turning point in your path to success.

Segmenting and targeting your email campaigns with ChatGPT

As an aspiring millionaire, you understand the importance of getting your message across to the right people. Segmentation and targeting are the keys to unlocking a world of increased conversions and revenue, and ChatGPT is your trusty guide on this journey.

Picture this: Your email campaigns are now tailored to each audience segment's unique needs and preferences. You've become a master at identifying your audience's various demographics, interests, and behaviors. With the help of ChatGPT, you're crafting content that resonates with each group, leading to sky-high engagement rates. Your conversions and income will soar as your targeted email campaigns gain traction. You'll leave your competitors in the dust, wondering how you created such powerful and personalized email campaigns. The secret, of course, is ChatGPT.

Embrace this cutting-edge technology and watch your email marketing strategy transform into a well-oiled machine, effortlessly generating income as you cater to the individual needs of your audience segments. The future of email marketing is here, and ChatGPT powers it.

You can ask, "How can I use ChatGPT to effectively segment and target my email campaigns, ensuring that my content is tailored to each audience's unique needs and preferences?" or "What specific strategies can I employ to optimize my segmented and targeted email campaigns using ChatGPT, and how will these improvements impact my overall engagement rates, conversions, and revenue?"

Remember to wield the incredible power of ChatGPT for segmenting and targeting your email campaigns. With the perfect blend of audience insights and AI-generated content, you'll be unstoppable. And as your income swells, you'll know that it was ChatGPT that helped you unlock the true potential of your email marketing strategy. Now, conquer the email marketing world with the unwavering confidence of a tech-savvy trailblazer!

Social Media Marketing and ChatGPT

Generating captivating social media content

Picture your social media profiles as a hub of excitement and engagement, filled with eye-catching content that your audience can't resist sharing. With ChatGPT by your side, you'll create captivating posts that resonate with your followers and amplify your online presence, driving traffic to your website and boosting conversions.

As an ambitious millionaire-in-the-making, you recognize the untapped potential of using AI-generated content to elevate your social media marketing game. ChatGPT empowers you to experiment with various content formats and styles, ensuring your posts remain fresh, diverse, and appealing to your audience.

You can ask, "How can I use ChatGPT to create a diverse range of captivating social media content that resonates with my audience and keeps them engaged?" or "What are the best strategies to leverage AI-generated content for driving traffic, boosting conversions, and increasing revenue through social media marketing?"

The more engaging your content, the more likely your followers will interact with your brand, share your posts, and convert into loyal customers. With the help of ChatGPT, you'll see your revenue soar as your social media profiles transform into powerful marketing machines.

Harness the power of AI to keep your audience hooked, and they'll reward you with their attention, loyalty, and, ultimately, their wallets. As your social media presence grows and your brand becomes synonymous with irresistible content, you'll be well on your way to achieving your millionaire dreams.

Just ask ChatGPT, "In what ways can I harness the power of ChatGPT to maintain a strong and engaging social media presence that contributes to customer loyalty and increased income?" or "How can I combine my marketing instincts with AI technology like ChatGPT to optimize my social media strategy and achieve greater success in my journey toward wealth?"

So, as you continue your journey toward wealth and success, keep ChatGPT at the forefront of your social media marketing strategy. The fusion of cutting-edge AI technology and your savvy marketing instincts will pave the way for a prosperous future. And when people ask how you managed to dominate the social media landscape, you can proudly respond, "I had a little help from my AI friend, ChatGPT."

Streamlining hashtag research and trend analysis

Imagine skyrocketing your social media reach and becoming a millionaire by leveraging the power of hashtags and trends. With ChatGPT, you can optimize your social media marketing strategy, boosting the visibility of your content and connecting with a broader audience.

You understand the importance of staying ahead of the curve. In no place other than social media hashtags, does the curve bend upwards with a new trend. ChatGPT can help you analyze trends and identify relevant, popular hashtags to include in your posts. This AI-driven approach ensures that your brand remains at the forefront of social media conversations, engaging with users and fostering a strong online presence.

You can ask, "How can I use ChatGPT to identify the most relevant and popular hashtags for my social media content, ensuring maximum visibility and reach?" or "What strategies can ChatGPT provide for effectively analyzing trends and incorporating them into my social media marketing approach to boost engagement and audience growth?"

ChatGPT's capabilities extend beyond mere hashtag research. It can also help you create timely, trend-driven content, positioning your brand as a thought leader in your industry. As your content gains traction, you'll witness an uptick in your reach, engagement, and, ultimately, your income.

The secret to your success? Capitalizing on the power of AI-generated insights, transforming your social media marketing game, and setting you on a path to riches. With ChatGPT, you'll have the ultimate tool to elevate your social media strategy, outshine your competition, and dominate the digital landscape.

Try asking, "In what ways can ChatGPT help me create timely, trend-driven content that positions my brand as a thought leader in my industry, leading to increased income?" or "How can I leverage ChatGPT's AI-generated insights to elevate my social media strategy, outperform my competition, and achieve my millionaire goals?"

With its cutting-edge AI capabilities, you'll be unstoppable, propelling your brand to new heights and making your marketing dreams a reality. And when your success story is written, don't forget to mention the invaluable role of ChatGPT in your journey, proving that even the most ambitious dreams can come true with the help of AI.

Crafting persuasive ad copy for social media campaigns

Picture yourself becoming one of the most well-known social media accounts through the power of compelling social media ad-copy. ChatGPT can be your secret weapon in creating captivating advertisements that drive your audience to act and contribute to your financial success.

Harness the potential of AI-generated ad copy to enhance your social media advertising campaigns. By utilizing ChatGPT, you can create persuasive ads that resonate with your audience, resulting in higher click-through rates and better conversions. This approach will save you time and resources, freeing you to focus on other aspects of your business. As an aspiring millionaire, you know that every click counts. With ChatGPT, you can craft ads that evoke emotion and urgency, leading your audience to take the desired action. Whether it's purchasing your product or signing up for your newsletter, effective ad copy can significantly impact your bottom line.

With ChatGPT's assistance, you'll be well on your way to reaping the rewards of your social media advertising efforts. Your brand will stand out among the competition, driving more traffic to your website and, ultimately, increasing your revenue.

You can ask, "How can I effectively use ChatGPT to create captivating and persuasive ad copy for my social media campaigns, resulting in higher click-through rates and increased revenue?" or "What are some specific strategies and techniques ChatGPT can provide to help me craft emotion-evoking ads that resonate with my audience, boosting my brand's visibility and my journey towards becoming a millionaire?"

Prepare to watch your conversions soar, and your bank account grows as you tap into the boundless potential of AI-generated ad copy. As your fortune flourishes, you'll look back and appreciate the crucial role ChatGPT played in your journey. And when it's time to celebrate your success, why not raise a glass to the AI-powered wonder that helped turn your dreams into reality? Cheers to ChatGPT!

Analyzing and Optimizing Performance

Monitoring key performance indicators (KPIs)

Monitoring KPIs is essential for evaluating the success of your marketing campaigns and making data-driven decisions. ChatGPT can assist you in tracking and analyzing essential KPIs, such as website traffic, conversion rates, click-through rates, and social media engagement.

By leveraging AI-generated insights, you can quickly identify the strengths and weaknesses of your marketing efforts, allowing you to make informed decisions about where to invest your resources. As a result, you can optimize your marketing strategy, drive better results, and generate more income through various revenue streams.

Millionaires know the value of data-driven decisions, and with ChatGPT's help, you can unlock the full potential of monitoring KPIs. Imagine the thrill of watching your marketing campaigns soar to new heights thanks to AI-generated insights on crucial KPIs like website traffic, conversion rates, click-through rates, and social media engagement.

You can quickly get a quality answer by asking, "How can ChatGPT assist me in tracking and analyzing essential KPIs to evaluate the success of my marketing campaigns?" or "What AI-generated insights can ChatGPT provide to help me identify the strengths and weaknesses of my marketing efforts and allocate resources effectively?"

As you dive into the data, ChatGPT empowers you to identify the strengths and weaknesses of your marketing efforts with laser-like precision. No more guessing games: you can pinpoint exactly where to invest your resources for maximum impact. With the power of AI-generated KPI analysis at your fingertips, you can optimize your marketing strategy like never before. The results will speak for themselves: better performance, increased revenue streams, and the satisfaction of knowing you're making the most of every marketing dollar.

You can ask, "How can I use ChatGPT's AI-generated KPI analysis to optimize my marketing strategy and achieve better performance across various revenue streams?" or "What specific ways can ChatGPT support my journey towards being a millionaire by providing data-driven insights for digital marketing success?"

Think of ChatGPT as your trusty sidekick, providing you with the data-driven insights you need to conquer digital marketing. So, strap on your metaphorical jetpack and prepare to blast off into a world of optimized marketing performance. As you rocket skyward, remember to give a cheeky salute to the AI that helped make it all possible: ChatGPT, the ultimate marketing partner for aspiring millionaires everywhere.

Gaining insights from sentiment analysis

Understanding your customers' opinions and emotions is crucial for improving your marketing campaigns and tailoring your content to their needs. ChatGPT can help you conduct sentiment analysis and gather valuable feedback from your customers by analyzing comments, reviews, and social media interactions.

By tapping into AI-generated insights, you can gain a deeper understanding of your target audience's preferences and pain points, allowing you to create more targeted and effective marketing campaigns. Ultimately, this will lead to increased customer satisfaction, higher conversion rates, and more revenue generation opportunities. Picture yourself as a millionaire, having harnessed the power of ChatGPT to perform sentiment analysis, unlocking a goldmine of insights into your customers' opinions and emotions. Imagine the exhilaration of taking your marketing campaigns to new heights by truly understanding your target audience, giving you the edge over competitors. Many people are already doing this.

Just ask, "How can ChatGPT help me conduct sentiment analysis to better understand my customers' opinions and emotions from comments, reviews, and social media interactions?" or "What specific AI-generated insights can ChatGPT provide to help me gain a deeper understanding of my target audience's preferences and pain points?"

With ChatGPT's AI-generated sentiment analysis, you'll be able to dive deep into customer feedback, pinpointing their preferences and pain points like never before. No more shooting in the dark – you'll have the knowledge to create laser-focused marketing campaigns that resonate with your audience and drive results.

By implementing the insights gained from sentiment analysis, you'll see customer satisfaction skyrocket, conversion rates climb, and revenue generation opportunities multiply. As you forge ahead on your path to financial freedom, you'll marvel at the way AI has transformed your marketing strategy, making it more agile, responsive, and, above all, profitable.

Ask ChatGPT, "How can ChatGPT help me conduct sentiment analysis to better understand my customers' opinions and emotions from comments, reviews, and social media interactions?" or "What specific AI-generated insights can ChatGPT provide to help me gain a deeper understanding of my target audience's preferences and pain points?"

So, as you dominate the marketing landscape with your newfound wisdom, remember to give a nod of gratitude to the AI sidekick that made it all possible: ChatGPT, the ultimate sentiment analysis partner. And as you celebrate your success, why not toast to the power of AI with a glass of champagne poured by your robot butler? Cheers to the future of marketing!

Adapting and refining your marketing strategy

The rapidly changing digital landscape requires businesses to constantly adapt and refine their marketing strategies to stay ahead of the competition. ChatGPT can provide valuable insights into your marketing campaigns' performance, helping you identify areas for improvement and uncover new opportunities.

By incorporating AI-generated insights into your decision-making process, you can optimize your marketing strategy, ensuring that your efforts are aligned with your target audience's needs and preferences. This will result in better engagement, increased website traffic, and higher conversion rates, generating more income through various monetization methods.

A great expert prompt to use is, "Discuss the role of ChatGPT in providing valuable insights into the performance of your marketing campaigns and explain how incorporating these insights into your decision-making process can lead to an optimized marketing strategy." or "Explore the advantages of using ChatGPT to continuously adapt and refine your marketing strategy in the rapidly changing digital landscape."

Imagine being on the fast track to becoming a millionaire by constantly adapting and refining your marketing strategy with the help of ChatGPT. The digital world moves at lightning speed, and you must stay ahead of the competition. That's where ChatGPT comes into play, providing you with invaluable insights and data to make informed decisions about your marketing campaigns.

With ChatGPT's AI-generated insights at your fingertips, you can optimize your marketing strategy like a pro, ensuring that your efforts align with the ever-evolving needs and preferences of your target audience. This continuous optimization will increase engagement, website traffic, and conversion rates, pushing you closer to that winning title. By leveraging the power of ChatGPT, you'll be in the driver's seat, steering your marketing campaigns towards unprecedented success. Your competitors will watch in awe as you navigate the digital landscape with finesse, leaving them in the dust as you secure your place among the marketing elite.

As you revel in your newfound success, take a moment to consider the future of marketing. Who knows, maybe someday you'll attend exclusive marketing conferences on Mars, chatting with fellow AI-assisted marketing millionaires as you discuss the latest breakthroughs in ChatGPT technology. Until then, keep optimizing, adapting, and refining your strategy.

Chapter 9: Virtual Assistant Services Powered by AI

Understanding the Role of AI as a VA

The Evolution of virtual assistants and AI Integration

The evolution of virtual assistants and AI integration has significantly changed the landscape of virtual assistant services. Traditionally, virtual assistants were human professionals who provided remote support to businesses and entrepreneurs.

However, with AI technologies like ChatGPT, virtual assistants have evolved into a powerful combination of human expertise and AI capabilities. This integration has led to more efficient and cost-effective services, enabling businesses to access high-quality support while saving time and resources.

The world of virtual assistant services has been revolutionized with the integration of AI technologies like ChatGPT. This powerful union of human expertise and AI capabilities has transformed the way businesses access high-quality support while saving time and resources. Imagine the possibilities of capitalizing on this lucrative industry, positioning yourself as a pioneer in AI-powered virtual assistant services, and making your millionaire dreams come true.

You can ask ChatGPT, "What are some examples of how AI-powered virtual assistants like ChatGPT can offer more efficient and cost-effective services compared to traditional human VAs?" or "How can I effectively integrate ChatGPT into my virtual assistant services to provide high-quality support while saving time and resources?"

Embracing ChatGPT as a virtual assistant not only enables you to provide faster and more accurate services to your clients, but also opens new revenue streams for your business. By offering AI-powered services, you can scale your business exponentially, serving a larger client base without the need to hire and manage an extensive team of human virtual assistants. This means lower overhead costs, higher profit margins, and an edge over your competitors who are still relying on traditional virtual assistant models.

The integration of AI in virtual assistant services is your ticket to building a thriving business and reaching your financial goals. As you leverage the power of ChatGPT, you'll be able to offer innovative and cutting-edge services, attracting high-profile clients who are eager to tap into the efficiency and cost-effectiveness of AI-powered support.

You can ask, "What strategies can I use to scale my AI-powered virtual assistant business and serve a larger client base without increasing overhead costs?" or "How can I market my AI-powered virtual assistant services to attract high-profile clients and stay ahead of competitors relying on traditional VA models?"

As you continue to expand your AI-powered virtual assistant empire, picture yourself sipping on an exotic beverage while lounging on your private island, surrounded by a team of AI-powered robots catering to your every whim. Your success story will become the stuff of legend, inspiring future generations to embrace the power of AI and follow in your footsteps. So, take the leap, harness the potential of ChatGPT, and turn your money-making aspirations into reality!

The benefits of using ChatGPT as a virtual assistant

The benefits of using ChatGPT as a virtual assistant are numerous. Incorporating AI into your virtual assistant services can provide faster and more accurate client support. ChatGPT can help with tasks such as content creation, proofreading, research, and data analysis, enabling you to offer a wider range of services and cater to diverse client needs.

By streamlining processes and automating repetitive tasks, ChatGPT allows you to focus on more complex tasks and expand your business, increasing revenue and growth.

Embracing the benefits of ChatGPT as a virtual assistant can propel you towards your dreams. As you tap into its capabilities to offer faster, more accurate support to your clients, you'll quickly become your niche's go-to virtual assistant service provider. With ChatGPT by your side, handling tasks like content creation, proofreading, research, and data analysis, you'll be able to cater to diverse client needs and secure high-profile contracts.

Capitalizing on the AI-powered virtual assistant market can help you scale your business and increase revenue. As you automate repetitive tasks and streamline processes, you'll free up time to focus on more complex tasks and building valuable client relationships. This, in turn, will open the doors to expanding your service offerings, catering to more industries, and growing your business exponentially.

You can ask, "What are the key benefits of using ChatGPT as a virtual assistant in terms of providing faster and more accurate support, and how can these benefits contribute to business growth and increased revenue?" or "How can I leverage ChatGPT's capabilities in tasks like content creation, proofreading, research, and data analysis to expand my virtual assistant service offerings and cater to diverse client needs in different industries?"

Imagine the possibilities as your AI-powered virtual assistant empire flourishes. You'll attract clients who recognize the value of utilizing ChatGPT's advanced capabilities, leading to a steady stream of lucrative projects. Your competitors will watch in awe as you effortlessly scale your business, and your success will become the envy of the industry.

Identifying the ideal client base for AI-powered virtual assistant services

Identifying the ideal client base for AI-powered virtual assistant services is crucial for maximizing your potential earnings. Businesses and entrepreneurs who require support in content creation, marketing, administrative tasks, and research are prime candidates for your services.

By targeting clients who value efficiency, accuracy, and innovation, you can establish a strong reputation as a virtual assistant who leverages cutting-edge technology like ChatGPT to deliver exceptional results. This competitive edge will help you attract more clients and generate higher income from your AI-powered virtual assistant services.

Zeroing in on the ideal client base for AI-powered virtual assistant services is your ticket to joining the millionaire's club. Clients like startups, e-commerce businesses, digital marketers, and busy entrepreneurs are hungry for innovative solutions that save them time, money, and effort. By delivering impeccable support using ChatGPT, you'll have them clamoring for your services.

Ask, "What types of businesses and entrepreneurs would benefit most from AI-powered virtual assistant services, and how can I tailor my offerings to cater to their unique needs?" or "How can I leverage ChatGPT's capabilities to establish a strong reputation for efficiency, accuracy, and innovation within my target client base?"

Picture yourself collaborating with thought leaders and industry giants, all eager to harness the power of AI to streamline their operations. As you confidently tackle their content creation, marketing, administrative, and research needs with ChatGPT's assistance, you'll quickly build a loyal client base that will serve as the foundation of your million-dollar empire.

As you attract clients from diverse industries and backgrounds, your virtual assistant services will become synonymous with innovation and efficiency. Your growing reputation as a ChatGPT-savvy virtual assistant will spread like wildfire, opening new opportunities for collaboration and partnerships, and catapulting you towards world recognition.

Ask ChatGPT, "What strategies can I use to effectively market my AI-powered virtual assistant services to thought leaders and industry giants across diverse industries?" or "What are some companies that I can approach that might want to leverage the ChatGPT API and have their own virtual assistants?"

Imagine the satisfaction of watching your bank account grow as you effortlessly handle project after project with ChatGPT's help. You'll be able to scale your business, hire a team of like-minded professionals, and continue expanding your client base, all while maintaining a work-life balance that others can only dream of.

Administrative Support with ChatGPT

Managing schedules and appointments using AI

Managing schedules and appointments using AI has revolutionized the way businesses operate. With ChatGPT's assistance, virtual assistants can efficiently handle their clients' calendars and appointments by setting up reminders, scheduling meetings, and coordinating events.

This level of automation saves time for both the virtual assistant and the client and reduces the risk of human error. Consequently, offering AI-powered scheduling and appointment management services can attract more clients and boost your revenue as a virtual assistant.

Imagine the sheer joy of clients who can trust their virtual assistants to manage their schedules and appointments flawlessly. With ChatGPT's AI capabilities, you'll offer administrative support that will have them raving about your services to their peers. As word spreads, you'll find yourself catering to the needs of high-profile clients who demand nothing less than perfection. And as a result, your earnings will skyrocket.

It's easy to ask something like, "How can I use ChatGPT to efficiently manage my clients' calendars, appointments, and events, while ensuring a high level of accuracy and customer satisfaction?" or "What strategies can I employ to market my AI-powered scheduling and appointment management services, attracting more clients and boosting my revenue?"

With ChatGPT handling the nitty-gritty of scheduling and appointments, you can focus on expanding your virtual assistant business. As you add more clients to your roster, you'll also be building a reputation as a reliable and innovative service provider. The more successful you have, the more your millionaire dreams become achievable.

Imagine your AI-powered business growing exponentially, with ChatGPT managing schedules and appointments for top executives, celebrities, and influencers. Your services will be in such high demand that you'll have the luxury of cherry-picking the most lucrative and prestigious clients. As your income soars, you'll be well on your way to joining the exclusive millionaire club easier than everyone who ever got there before you.

Use a great prompt such as "How can I use ChatGPT to efficiently manage my clients' calendars, appointments, and events, while ensuring a high level of accuracy and customer satisfaction?" or "What strategies can I employ to market my AI-powered scheduling and appointment management services, attracting more clients and boosting my revenue?"

And as you revel in your success, you'll be able to invest in further growth and expansion of your business. You'll diversify your service offerings, attract a team of like-minded professionals, and continue to leverage ChatGPT's power to elevate your business. The sky's the limit when it comes to the potential of AI-powered administrative support.

Streamlining email management and response

Streamlining email management and response with ChatGPT is another valuable service you can offer to your clients. ChatGPT can help you draft professional and well-structured email responses, ensuring timely and effective communication on behalf of your clients.

By leveraging AI to manage your clients' inboxes, you can quickly sort through emails, prioritize messages, and provide prompt replies. This efficiency level will appeal to busy clients who need assistance with email management, ultimately leading to increased demand for your virtual assistant services and higher earnings.

When it comes to making serious money as an AI-powered virtual assistant, streamlining email management and response with ChatGPT is a game-changer. The more efficient and professional your email support services are, the more high-profile clients will be clamoring to work with you. And that's when the real magic happens – as you build a reputation for impeccable email management, your earnings will soar.

You can quickly ask, "How can I use Python and the ChatGPT API to draft professional email responses including sorting and prioritizing messages?" or "What strategies can I use to market my AI-powered email management services to attract busy clients who need assistance in this area?"

Imagine being known as the go-to virtual assistant for managing email correspondence for some of the most influential business magnates and celebrities. By tapping into ChatGPT's AI capabilities, you'll be able to craft compelling and persuasive email responses, ensuring your clients' inboxes stay organized and their communication stays on point.

As your reputation for effective email management grows, you'll be able to command top-dollar rates for your services. Clients will gladly pay a premium for the peace of mind that comes with knowing their email communications are in the hands of a true professional who utilizes cutting-edge AI technology. And as you rake in those lucrative fees, your newfound wealth tree will inch ever closer.

For another great prompt ask, "How can I leverage my reputation for effective email management to command higher rates and attract high-profile clients for my AI-powered virtual assistant services?" or "What steps should I take to refine and expand my AI-powered email management services, further establishing my virtual assistant empire and catering to the needs of successful individuals?"

Your journey to the millionaire club doesn't stop there, though. By continuously refining and expanding your AI-powered email management services, you'll attract even more top-tier clients. This will fuel your growth and help you establish an elite virtual assistant empire, catering to the email management needs of the world's most successful individuals.

Organizing documents, files, and data using AI-generated insights

Organizing documents, files, and data using AI-generated insights is a game-changing service you can provide as a virtual assistant. ChatGPT can help you analyze and categorize documents, streamline file management, and even generate reports or summaries.

By offering this type of AI-powered document and data organization service, you can help clients save time, reduce clutter, and make better-informed decisions based on the insights generated by ChatGPT. As a result, you'll be able to expand your client base, increase your income, and establish yourself as a virtual assistant who harnesses the power of AI to deliver top-notch support.

When it comes to building a millionaire virtual assistant business, offering AI-powered document organization services can set you on the path to riches. Harnessing the power of ChatGPT to help clients manage their documents, files, and data will improve their productivity and showcase your innovative approach to administrative support. This, in turn, will help you gain a competitive edge and attract a high-paying clientele.

You can ask, "How can I use ChatGPT to analyze, categorize, and streamline document and file organization for my clients, and what kind of reports or summaries can I generate with it?" or "What strategies can I use to scale my AI-powered document and data organization services to potential clients who value efficiency and innovation?"

The secret to unlocking your millionaire potential lies in the efficiency and accuracy of your document organization services. ChatGPT can help you quickly analyze and categorize large volumes of files, making it easy for clients to find what they need when they need it. By incorporating AI-generated insights into your document organization process, you'll create a system that adapts and improves over time, ensuring that your clients' digital spaces remain impeccably organized.

As you build a reputation for exceptional document organization, clients will flock to your services. This will allow you to charge premium rates, bringing you closer to achieving your entrepreneurial dreams. And the best part? The more clients you attract, the more you can refine and expand your AI-powered document organization services, keeping your business on the cutting edge and pushing your income even higher.

With ChatGPT just ask, "How can I refine and expand my AI-powered document organization services to ensure that I remain on the cutting edge and continue to attract high-paying clients?" or "What steps should I take to maintain impeccable document organization for my clients while adapting and improving my system over time using AI-generated insights?"

So, as you embark on this journey to millionaire status, remember that the secret to your success lies in the power of AI-generated insights and document organization. As your virtual assistant empire grows, you'll look back on this moment and realize that ChatGPT was the secret weapon that helped you conquer the world of document organization.

Content Creation Services with ChatGPT

Writing blog posts, articles, and social media content

Writing blog posts, articles, and social media content using AI assistance is a powerful way to elevate your virtual assistant services. ChatGPT can help you produce engaging, well-written, and SEO-optimized content for your clients, enabling you to take on more projects and increase your income.

By leveraging AI to create high-quality content, you can save time, reduce writer's block, and ensure a consistent flow of work for your clients. This added value will attract more clients seeking top-notch content creation services, resulting in higher earnings for you as a virtual assistant.

Want to become a millionaire virtual assistant? I mean do you REALLY want to reach that status. You do! Ok, well focus on offering top-notch content creation services using ChatGPT, and watch your business take off like a rocket. With AI assistance, you can quickly generate blog posts, articles, and social media content that resonates with your clients' target audience, leaving them coming back for more.

You can ask, "How can I use the ChatGPT API to create engaging and SEO-optimized blog posts, articles, and social media content for my clients via their WordPress JSON post?" or "How can I effectively market my AI-assisted content creation services to attract more clients and increase my income as a virtual assistant?"

Using ChatGPT to create content is like having a secret weapon in your arsenal. Say goodbye to writer's block and hello to an endless stream of engaging, shareable, and SEO-friendly content. As you continue to impress your clients with high-quality content produced with AI assistance, word of mouth will spread like wildfire, attracting even more clients to your virtual doorstep.

So, how can you level up your content creation game and tap into that millionaire mindset? First, hone your skills in using ChatGPT to generate various types of content, from informative blog posts to snappy social media captions. Next, stay updated on the latest SEO best practices and incorporate them into your content creation process. This will ensure that the content you create is not only engaging but also primed for maximum visibility on search engines and social media platforms.

As your content creation services gain traction and your clientele grows, consider scaling your virtual assistant business by outsourcing some of the work to other talented freelancers. This will allow you to take on even more projects, skyrocketing your income and inching you ever closer to your millionaire goal.

You can ask ChatGPT, "How can I continuously improve my content creation skills using ChatGPT and stay updated on the latest SEO best practices to ensure maximum visibility for my clients' content?" or "What strategies should I consider when scaling my virtual assistant business and outsourcing work to other freelancers to accommodate more content creation projects and increase my income?"

Thanks to your AI-assisted content creation prowess, you might just feel like shouting from the rooftops, "I am the content king, and ChatGPT is my royal scribe!" So, strap in and get ready for the thrilling ride to the top of the virtual assistant world, fueled by the power of ChatGPT and your unrelenting drive to succeed.

Proofreading and editing content with ChatGPT's support

Proofreading and editing content with ChatGPT's support is another valuable offering in your virtual assistant toolkit. ChatGPT can identify and correct grammatical errors, improve sentence structure, and suggest better word choices, ensuring your clients receive polished, professional content.

By incorporating AI into your proofreading and editing process, you can deliver error-free work more efficiently and take on a higher volume of projects. This increased productivity will appeal to clients and ultimately boost your revenue as a virtual assistant specializing in content creation.

Imagine if you could turn the dial up on your virtual assistant business and watch your income soar by offering top tier proofreading and editing services. Well, with ChatGPT by your side, that dream can become a reality. This AI-powered tool can significantly enhance your proofreading and editing capabilities, making your services even more attractive to clients.

A great prompt to use is, "What are some effective techniques for using ChatGPT to proofread and edit content, ensuring error-free and polished results for my clients?" or "How can I market my AI-assisted proofreading and editing services to attract more clients and increase my income as a virtual assistant?"

The secret to earning big with ChatGPT's proofreading and editing support lies in its ability to swiftly identify grammatical errors, tighten up sentence structure, and suggest more precise word choices. This means that you can deliver polished, professional content that will leave clients impressed and eager to work with you again.

To fully harness the potential of ChatGPT in proofreading and editing, make sure to familiarize yourself with its various features and capabilities. This way, you'll be able to quickly spot and correct errors, resulting in faster turnaround times for your projects. Your clients will appreciate the efficiency, and you'll be able to take on more work, catapulting your income to new heights.

You can ask, "How can I stay current with the latest style guides and industry standards to ensure the content I proofread and edit meets my clients' expectations?" or "What strategies can I use to improve my proofreading and editing efficiency with ChatGPT, allowing me to take on more projects and boost my income?"

Additionally, stay up to date with the latest style guides and industry standards to ensure the content you deliver adheres to your clients' specifications. By combining your knowledge of best practices with ChatGPT's proofreading and editing capabilities, you'll become a force to be reckoned with in the virtual assistant world.

Generating creative ideas and brainstorming

Generating creative ideas and brainstorming with AI input is an innovative way to expand your virtual assistant services. ChatGPT can help you come up with unique ideas for blog posts, marketing campaigns, or product development for your clients. By tapping into AI-generated insights, you can offer a fresh perspective and provide valuable input to your clients' projects.

This creative edge will set you apart from other virtual assistants, allowing you to attract a diverse range of clients and increase your income. By offering AI-powered brainstorming and ideation services, you can position yourself as a cutting-edge virtual assistant who delivers exceptional results.

Picture yourself as the go-to virtual assistant for brainstorming and idea generation, all because you've harnessed the power of ChatGPT. It's not just a pipe dream; it's an attainable goal that can propel your income to the millionaire level. With AI-driven insights, you'll be able to provide clients with fresh, innovative ideas that will leave them amazed and eager for more.

You can ask, "What are some techniques for using ChatGPT to generate unique and creative ideas for blog posts, marketing campaigns, or product development for my clients?" or "How can I effectively market my AI-assisted brainstorming and idea generation services to attract more clients and increase my income as a virtual assistant?"

When you team up with ChatGPT for brainstorming, you'll be able to quickly generate a plethora of unique ideas for blog posts, marketing campaigns, or product development. This ability to rapidly produce creative solutions will make you an invaluable asset to your clients, helping you secure more work and boost your income.

To make the most of ChatGPT's ideation capabilities, familiarize yourself with its features and learn how to fine-tune the AI's output for optimal results. As you gain expertise in using ChatGPT for brainstorming, you'll develop a reputation for providing ingenious solutions, drawing in a diverse range of clients, and expanding your income streams.

A great to use prompt is, "What are some strategies for fine-tuning ChatGPT's output to produce optimal brainstorming results that will impress my clients?" or "How can I stay informed about the latest trends and developments in my clients' [your niche] industry to ensure the ideas I generate with ChatGPT are relevant and timely?"

Another essential element of success in offering AI-powered brainstorming services is staying informed about the latest trends and developments in your clients' industries. This knowledge, combined with ChatGPT's insights, will enable you to propose relevant and timely ideas that will resonate with your clients and their target audiences.

Marketing and Social Media Management

Developing marketing strategies and campaigns

Developing marketing strategies and campaigns with AI-generated insights is a powerful way to elevate your virtual assistant services in the marketing domain. ChatGPT can provide data-driven recommendations and innovative ideas for marketing campaigns, helping you create more effective strategies for your clients.

By incorporating AI insights into your marketing efforts, you can deliver better results, improve your clients' ROI, and ultimately increase your income as a virtual assistant. Offering AI-powered marketing strategies will set you apart from competitors and make your services more attractive to potential clients. Embrace the future of marketing by harnessing the power of ChatGPT to create data-driven, innovative marketing strategies and campaigns for your clients. By leveraging AI-generated insights, you can deliver outstanding results that will boost your clients' ROI and set you on the path to becoming a real entrepreneurial virtual assistant.

You can easily ask, "What are some effective techniques for using ChatGPT to develop data-driven marketing strategies and campaigns that improve my clients' ROI?" or "How can I market my AI-assisted marketing strategy services to attract more clients and increase my income as a virtual assistant?"

ChatGPT can help you identify emerging trends and analyze consumer behavior, enabling you to craft targeted and effective marketing strategies for your clients. As a virtual assistant, you'll be able to devise campaigns that not only meet but exceed your clients' expectations, making your services indispensable and attracting a steady stream of new business.

To make the most of ChatGPT's marketing capabilities, invest time in learning how to fine-tune the AI's output and customize its recommendations to align with your clients' goals and target audiences. This will allow you to deliver tailored marketing solutions that will leave your clients in awe of your expertise.

You can ask the best A.I. "What are some effective techniques for using ChatGPT to develop data-driven marketing strategies and campaigns that improve my clients' ROI?" or "How can I market my AI-assisted marketing strategy services to attract more clients and increase my income as a virtual assistant?"

Additionally, staying up to date on the latest marketing techniques and industry trends will ensure you remain ahead of the competition. By combining your knowledge with ChatGPT's insights, you'll be able to create cutting-edge marketing strategies that will put you on the fast track to success.

Crafting, engaging social media content and managing accounts.

Crafting engaging social media content and managing accounts with the help of ChatGPT is another valuable service you can offer as a virtual assistant. ChatGPT can generate captivating post ideas, hashtags, and captions tailored to different platforms, allowing you to effectively manage your clients' social media presence.

By streamlining the social media management process using AI, you can save time and take on more clients, resulting in higher earnings. Your ability to consistently deliver high-quality, AI-assisted social media content will make your services more appealing and help you build a successful virtual assistant business.

Imagine the impact you can make as a virtual assistant by utilizing ChatGPT to craft engaging social media content and manage your clients' accounts! By mastering AI-assisted social media management, you'll be well on your way to becoming a virtual assistant that people remember.

You can use the prompt, "How can I use ChatGPT to generate captivating post ideas, hashtags, and captions that will help me effectively manage my clients' social media presence?" or "What strategies can I use to streamline the social media management process using AI, enabling me to save time and take on more clients?"

With ChatGPT's ability to generate captivating post ideas, hashtags, and captions, you can manage multiple clients' social media accounts with ease, expanding your business and increasing your income. By staying up to date with the latest social media trends and platform features, you'll be able to offer cutting-edge services that clients will eagerly seek out. To maximize your revenue potential, use ChatGPT's insights to create platform-specific content that appeals to your clients' target audiences. This will help to grow their follower base and increase engagement, solidifying your reputation as a results-driven virtual assistant.

You can ask, "What are some tips for using ChatGPT to create platform-specific content that appeals to my clients' target audiences and grows their follower base?" or "How can I incorporate social media advertising and analytics services into my AI-assisted virtual assistant offerings to increase my value to clients?"

As you continue to hone your social media management skills, consider offering additional services, such as social media advertising and analytics. Combining ChatGPT's capabilities with your own expertise in these areas will make you an even more asset to your clients.

Analyzing marketing performance and optimizing campaigns

Analyzing marketing performance and optimizing campaigns using ChatGPT is an essential service for virtual assistants specializing in marketing. ChatGPT can help you track key performance indicators (KPIs), identify trends, and provide recommendations for improving your clients' marketing campaigns.

By leveraging AI-generated insights, you can make data-driven decisions and continuously refine your clients' marketing efforts. This added value will attract clients seeking top-notch marketing services and ultimately boost your revenue as a virtual assistant. Offering AI-powered marketing analysis and optimization will position you as a leading virtual assistant in the marketing field.

You can try asking, "How can I use ChatGPT to track key performance indicators (KPIs) and identify trends in my clients' marketing campaigns?" or "What recommendations can ChatGPT provide for improving my clients' marketing efforts and optimizing their campaigns?"

Get ready to skyrocket your virtual assistant business by harnessing the power of ChatGPT to analyze marketing performance and optimize campaigns! As an aspiring millionaire virtual assistant, it's time to delve into AI-generated insights to make data-driven decisions and refine your clients' marketing efforts.

Utilize ChatGPT to track KPIs, identify trends, and provide actionable recommendations to improve your clients' marketing campaigns. By doing so, you'll create a virtuous cycle of performance improvement, leading to increased client satisfaction, loyalty, and word-of-mouth referrals. To maximize the effectiveness of your AI-powered marketing analysis and optimization, stay current with industry best practices and emerging technologies. This way, you'll be able to combine ChatGPT's insights with your expertise to create a winning strategy for your clients.

You can ask ChatGPT, "How can I stay current with industry best practices and emerging technologies to maximize the effectiveness of AI-powered marketing analysis and optimization?" or "What strategies can I use to scale my virtual assistant business and teach team members to effectively utilize ChatGPT?"

By offering AI-powered marketing analysis and optimization, you'll distinguish yourself from competitors, attract more clients, and achieve the financial freedom you've always dreamed of. And as your virtual assistant business grows, you'll be able to scale your services by teaching your team members how to utilize ChatGPT effectively.

Building and Scaling Your AI-Powered Business

Establishing your virtual assistant services

Establishing your virtual assistant services and pricing structure is crucial to building a successful AI-powered virtual assistant business. With ChatGPT's assistance, you can provide a wide range of services, including administrative support, content creation, marketing, and social media management. It's important to determine which services you'll offer and create a pricing structure that reflects the value you provide.

By leveraging ChatGPT's capabilities, you can enhance your offerings and justify premium pricing, ultimately increasing your income as a virtual assistant. A well-defined service offering and pricing structure will help you attract clients and generate consistent revenue.

Try asking with the prompt, "What are some strategies for creating a pricing structure that reflects the value of my AI-powered virtual assistant services?" or "How can I use ChatGPT to enhance my service offerings and justify premium pricing?"

Embrace your inner millionaire and establish your AI-powered virtual assistant services with ChatGPT! Focus on creating a well-defined service offering and pricing structure that showcases your unique value proposition. With ChatGPT's capabilities, you can enhance your offerings and justify premium pricing, putting you on the path to wealth.

To succeed in this highly competitive market, differentiate yourself by specializing in niches where ChatGPT shines. Emphasize the value that AI-powered services bring to your clients, such as increased efficiency, innovative ideas, and improved accuracy. This way, you'll make your services irresistible to potential clients. As your virtual assistant business grows, invest in marketing and networking to attract more clients. Showcase your AI-powered success stories through case studies, testimonials, and social media to build your reputation. Remember, word-of-mouth referrals are a powerful way to scale your business!

Another great prompt is, "What marketing and networking techniques can I use to attract more clients and showcase my AI-powered success stories?" or "How can I build a team of like-minded virtual assistants, train them in AI-powered services, and create a system for delivering consistent results?"

As you continue to expand, consider building a team of like-minded virtual assistants who can also leverage ChatGPT. Train them in AI-powered services and create a system that enables them to deliver consistent results. This way, you can take on more clients and projects, ultimately multiplying your revenue.

Marketing your AI-powered virtual assistant business

Marketing your AI-powered virtual assistant business is essential to attracting clients and growing your business. Utilizing ChatGPT for crafting persuasive marketing materials, such as email campaigns and social media posts, can significantly improve your marketing efforts.

Highlight the benefits of your AI-powered services, emphasizing the value you provide and how you stand out from traditional virtual assistants. By showcasing your unique selling points and the power of ChatGPT, you'll attract more clients and increase your revenue. Welcome to the world of millionaire marketing strategies for your AI-powered virtual assistant business! With ChatGPT, you can turbocharge your marketing efforts and create a powerful online presence that attracts high-paying clients.

You can ask, "What are some strategies for crafting persuasive marketing materials with ChatGPT for my AI-powered virtual assistant business?" or "How can I effectively showcase the unique benefits of my AI-powered services to attract more clients and get repeat customers totaling $10k a month?"

First, let's dive into the realm of content marketing. Utilize ChatGPT to produce top-notch blog posts, articles, and case studies that showcase your expertise and demonstrate the results you can deliver. Share these masterpieces across social media platforms and watch your credibility skyrocket! Next, conquer the email marketing world with ChatGPT's help. Craft irresistible subject lines, engaging copy, and persuasive calls-to-action that motivate potential clients to take the plunge and work with you. With ChatGPT, you'll send emails to leads that convert like crazy and rake in the revenue.

Don't forget about social media advertising! Use ChatGPT to create eye-catching ad copy and target the right audience to expand your reach. By leveraging AI-generated insights, you'll optimize your ad spend and attract clients who are ready to invest in your top-tier services.

You can ask ChatGPT, "How can I use ChatGPT to create engaging blog posts, articles, and case studies that demonstrate my expertise and the results I can deliver?" or "What are some AI-generated keyword suggestions and content optimization strategies to improve SEO for my AI-powered virtual assistant business?"

Finally, harness the power of SEO by incorporating AI-generated keyword suggestions and content optimization strategies. Watch as your AI-powered virtual assistant business ranks higher in search results, driving organic traffic and interested clients straight to your website.

Adapting and expanding your service offerings

Adapting and expanding your service offerings based on client needs and AI advancements is key to maintaining a competitive edge in the virtual assistant market. As AI technology continues to evolve, new capabilities and features will emerge, providing you with even more tools to enhance your services.

By staying up to date with the latest AI developments and adjusting your offerings accordingly, you'll continue to meet the ever-changing needs of your clients. This adaptability will ensure your AI-powered virtual assistant business remains relevant and profitable in the long run, allowing you to capitalize on the growing demand for AI-enhanced virtual assistant services.

You can ask, "What are some strategies for staying up to date with the latest AI developments and adjusting my service offerings accordingly?" or "How can I ensure my AI-powered virtual assistant business remains relevant and profitable as AI technology continues to evolve?"

Welcome to the fast-paced, ever-evolving world of AI-powered virtual assistant services! Embrace the excitement of expanding your service offerings and adapt to the latest AI advancements like a true millionaire. With ChatGPT by your side, you'll always be ahead of the curve, ready to capitalize on new opportunities and amaze your clients.

Stay alert for emerging AI trends and breakthroughs in natural language processing, data analysis, and automation. By keeping your finger on the pulse of AI advancements, you'll be the first to implement cutting-edge solutions for your clients, boosting your reputation and revenue. Imagine the thrill of unveiling a groundbreaking service that propels your business to new heights! Don't shy away from exploring niche markets where AI can make a difference. From industry-specific applications to specialized tasks, ChatGPT's ever-expanding capabilities will help you carve out lucrative niches that set you apart from the competition. You'll become the go-to virtual assistant for high-paying clients seeking top-notch, AI-powered solutions.

Just ask ChatGPT, "What are some emerging AI trends and breakthroughs in natural language processing, data analysis, and automation that I should be aware of as a virtual assistant?" or "How can I identify niche markets where AI can make a difference and leverage ChatGPT's capabilities to provide specialized solutions?"

Always keep an ear to the ground, listening to your clients' evolving needs and expectations. As you uncover new pain points and challenges, harness ChatGPT's power to develop innovative solutions that leave your clients in awe. The more you cater to their unique requirements, the more indispensable your services become.

Chapter 10: Stock Market and Investment Analysis

Understanding AI's Role in Analysis

The impact of AI on financial analysis and investment decision-making

Artificial intelligence has been transforming the financial industry by automating various aspects of analysis and decision-making. With AI-powered tools like ChatGPT, investors can process vast amounts of financial data quickly and accurately, enabling them to make more informed decisions. AI algorithms can identify patterns and trends that may be difficult for human analysts to discern, providing a competitive edge in investment decision-making.

Unlock the full potential of AI-powered financial analysis with ChatGPT and become the millionaire investor you've always dreamed of being. With ChatGPT's ability to crunch numbers and analyze complex data sets at lightning speed, you'll be making informed decisions and finding hidden opportunities in no time.

You can ask, "How can ChatGPT help me process and analyze large amounts of financial data to make more informed investment decisions?" or "What are some examples of patterns and trends that AI algorithms like ChatGPT can identify to provide a competitive edge in investment decision-making?"

Stay ahead of the curve by utilizing ChatGPT's prowess in spotting patterns and trends that mere mortals might miss. Imagine harnessing the power of AI to uncover lucrative investments, giving you the advantage, you need to outperform the market and watch your wealth multiply. Dive deep into the ocean of financial data with ChatGPT by your side. Whether it's analyzing balance sheets, income statements, or market sentiment, ChatGPT will help you navigate the treacherous waters of the stock market with confidence. You'll be the captain of your financial destiny, steering your portfolio towards unimaginable gains.

You can ask "What types of financial data can ChatGPT analyze to help me navigate the stock market more effectively and confidently?" or "How can I best combine ChatGPT's capabilities with my own intuition and experience to create a winning formula for investment success?"

Combine the power of ChatGPT with your own intuition and experience, creating a winning formula for investment success. Leverage AI's capabilities to enhance your decision-making process, but never forget the value of human judgment. Together, you and ChatGPT will become an unstoppable investing force, capable of conquering any financial challenge.

Benefits of using ChatGPT in investment analysis

ChatGPT offers numerous advantages for investment analysis. Its natural language processing capabilities allow it to digest and interpret complex financial documents and reports. This enables investors to gain valuable insights without spending countless hours reading through dense materials.

Additionally, ChatGPT can help generate investment ideas by analyzing market trends and offering suggestions based on the user's preferences and risk tolerance. By incorporating ChatGPT into their analysis process, investors can save time, reduce the risk of human error, and make more informed investment decisions.

To help, ask, "What are the key advantages of using ChatGPT in investment analysis, and how can it help me make better investment decisions?" or "How can ChatGPT assist me in generating investment ideas that align with my preferences and risk tolerance?"

Integrating AI into your investment strategy

To make the most of AI-powered tools like ChatGPT, investors need to integrate them into their overall investment strategy. This can be done by utilizing AI-generated insights to complement human intuition and experience, ensuring a well-rounded approach to decision-making.

Investors can also use ChatGPT to monitor market developments, analyze specific stocks or assets, and even generate investment thesis ideas. By incorporating AI-driven tools into their strategy, investors can stay ahead of market trends and capitalize on opportunities that may have otherwise gone unnoticed. When it comes to achieving your millionaire goals, nothing beats a master plan that seamlessly integrates AI into your investment strategy. With ChatGPT as your secret weapon, you'll supercharge your financial prowess and catapult yourself into the realm of the ultra-wealthy.

You can ask, "How can I effectively integrate AI-generated insights from ChatGPT into my overall investment strategy to make better decisions?" or "What are some specific ways I can use ChatGPT to monitor market developments and analyze stocks or assets?"

What I'm in the middle of building is a real time application that tracks stocks and uses ChatGPT to summarize the best news from a free stock RSS feed and advise users when to make a buy or sell decision. You can combine the power of ChatGPT with your own intuition and experience and create a formidable approach to decision-making. Think of it as the perfect blend of human ingenuity and AI-driven insights, working in harmony to maximize your investment returns. With ChatGPT by your side, you can stay ahead of market developments and seize opportunities that others might miss. It's like having your own personal financial crystal ball, showing you the path to success in the ever-changing world of investments.

ChatGPT can also help you dive deep into the analysis of specific stocks or assets, ensuring that no stone is left unturned in your quest for financial triumph. Gone are the days of manual research and number crunching – with AI at your disposal, you'll be making investment decisions with confidence and precision.

Just ask ChatGPT, "How can ChatGPT help me stay ahead of market developments and identify opportunities others might miss?" or "What are the benefits of combining human expertise with AI technology like ChatGPT in my investment strategy?"

By incorporating AI-driven tools into your investment strategy, you'll be riding the wave of innovation that's transforming the financial landscape. As you watch your wealth multiply, you'll know that it's the perfect fusion of human expertise and AI technology that's propelling you to new heights.

Ai Powered Market Research and Data Analysis

Leveraging ChatGPT for market research and stock screening

ChatGPT can be an invaluable tool for conducting market research and stock screening. By processing large amounts of data, it can help identify potential investment opportunities based on specific criteria, such as industry, market cap, or dividend yield. Investors can save time and effort by using ChatGPT to analyze and filter stocks, allowing them to focus on high-potential opportunities.

This efficient approach to market research and stock screening can be an essential factor in generating increased profits. Unleash the full power of ChatGPT in your pursuit of entrepreneurial vision, by leveraging its capabilities in market research and stock screening. Imagine a world where you have access to a tireless research assistant, working around the clock to uncover hidden gems in the stock market. That's the reality with ChatGPT by your side. This AI-driven approach to stock selection enables you to zero in on potential investment opportunities tailored to your specific criteria. Whether you're looking for high-growth stocks or reliable dividend payers, ChatGPT has got you covered. Its ability to sift through mountains of data with laser-like precision means that you'll never miss a golden opportunity again.

You can ask, "How can ChatGPT help me with market research and stock screening to identify potential investment opportunities based on my specific criteria?" or "What are the benefits of using ChatGPT for market research and stock screening in terms of time savings and investment returns?"

As a future millionaire, you know that time is money. Using ChatGPT for market research and stock screening not only saves you valuable time but also boosts your investment returns by focusing on high-potential stocks. This winning combination is what sets you apart from the competition, propelling you towards financial greatness.

Utilizing AI-generated insights for fundamental analysis

This involves evaluating a company's financial health and performance to determine its intrinsic value. ChatGPT can assist investors in this process by generating insights from financial statements, industry reports, and news articles.

By using ChatGPT to analyze factors such as revenue growth, profit margins, and debt levels, investors can gain a better understanding of a company's financial position and potential for growth. This comprehensive understanding, driven by AI-generated insights, can help investors make more informed decisions and maximize their returns.

In your quest for financial success, AI-generated insights can be the game-changer that sets you apart from the crowd. With ChatGPT at your disposal, you can unlock the true potential of fundamental analysis, unearthing the hidden value in stocks and propelling your investment returns to new heights.

Dive deep into the world of fundamental analysis, powered by ChatGPT's remarkable ability to process vast amounts of financial data. It's like having your personal financial oracle guiding you through the maze of company reports and industry trends to uncover the most promising investment opportunities. ChatGPT can dissect complex financial statements and industry reports, providing you with an edge in understanding the company's financial position and growth potential.

Just ask, "How can ChatGPT assist me in fundamental analysis by generating insights from financial statements, industry reports, and news articles?" or "What advantages do AI-generated insights provide when conducting fundamental analysis to make more informed investment decisions and maximize returns?"

Embrace the power of AI-generated insights and watch your portfolio soar to financial freedom. With ChatGPT by your side, you'll navigate the financial landscape with ease and confidence, making investment decisions that not only maximize your returns but also minimize risk.

Applying technical analysis with ChatGPT's assistance

Technical analysis is a popular method for evaluating investments based on historical price movements and trading patterns. With ChatGPT's assistance, investors can analyze complex chart patterns, trends, and indicators more efficiently.

By automating aspects of technical analysis, ChatGPT can help investors identify potential entry and exit points, as well as generate trading signals based on specific criteria. By incorporating AI-driven technical analysis into their investment strategy, investors can optimize their trading decisions and potentially boost their profits.

Technical analysis can be the key to unlocking a treasure trove of investment opportunities. With ChatGPT's assistance, you'll harness the power of AI to cut through the complexities of historical price movements and trading patterns. Unleash your inner millionaire by maximizing the potential of AI-driven technical analysis, optimizing your trading decisions, and boosting your profits. Imagine having an AI-driven crystal ball that can uncover hidden patterns and trends in the stock market, allowing you to capitalize on lucrative trading opportunities. ChatGPT is that crystal ball, providing you with the tools to make data-driven decisions and outperform the competition.

You can ask, "How can ChatGPT assist me in applying technical analysis to evaluate investments based on historical price movements and trading patterns?" or "What benefits can I gain from incorporating AI-driven technical analysis into my investment strategy to optimize trading decisions and boost profits?"

By incorporating AI-driven technical analysis into your investment strategy, you can identify potential entry and exit points with ease. ChatGPT can help you generate trading signals based on specific criteria, streamlining your trading decisions, and keeping you one step ahead of the market.

Portfolio Management and Risk Assessment

Building a diversified portfolio using AI-generated recommendations

A diversified portfolio can help investors minimize risk and enhance returns. ChatGPT can assist in building a well-rounded portfolio by providing AI-generated recommendations based on factors such as asset allocation, investment horizon, and risk tolerance. By analyzing an investor's preferences and financial goals, ChatGPT can suggest a tailored mix of investments, including stocks, bonds, and alternative assets.

This personalized approach to portfolio construction, powered by AI, can help investors make better investment decisions and ultimately increase their profits. Let's dive right into the heart of how ChatGPT can help you build a powerful, diversified portfolio to catapult you into realms of other millionaires. With AI-generated recommendations at your fingertips, you can tap into a vast pool of knowledge to create a personalized investment strategy that meets your unique goals and preferences.

You can ask, "How can ChatGPT help me create a diversified portfolio based on my risk tolerance, investment horizon, and preferences?" or "What specific recommendations can ChatGPT provide to optimize my portfolio's performance and minimize risk?"

Using cutting-edge AI technology, ChatGPT can assess your risk tolerance and investment horizon, guiding you to a tailored mix of investments such as stocks, bonds, and alternative assets. This ensures that your portfolio is not only diversified but also attuned to your specific needs and financial objectives.

By tapping into the power of AI-generated recommendations, you can optimize your portfolio's performance, striking the right balance between risk and reward. This data-driven approach allows you to make informed investment decisions, all while minimizing the impact of market volatility.

You can ask, "How can I use AI-generated recommendations to complement my own expertise and intuition in making investment decisions?" or "What strategies can I employ to refine my portfolio over time using ChatGPT's insights and suggestions?"

As you continue to refine your portfolio, remember that AI-generated recommendations are just one component of your overall strategy. Combining the insights provided by ChatGPT with your expertise and intuition can create a formidable investing force, setting you on the path to millionaire status.

Analyzing portfolio performance and risk with ChatGPT's support

Monitoring and evaluating portfolio performance is essential for any investor. ChatGPT can support this process by providing in-depth analysis of portfolio returns, volatility, and risk-adjusted performance metrics. By comparing these metrics against relevant benchmarks, investors can gauge their portfolio's effectiveness and identify areas for improvement.

Additionally, ChatGPT can help assess the overall risk of a portfolio by analyzing correlations between different assets and estimating potential losses during market downturns. This comprehensive risk assessment can guide investors in making necessary adjustments to optimize their portfolio and enhance their returns.

Just ask ChatGPT, "How can ChatGPT help me monitor and evaluate my portfolio's performance, including returns, volatility, and risk-adjusted metrics?" or "What insights can ChatGPT provide to help me identify areas for improvement in my portfolio in the energy sector?"

Harness the power of ChatGPT to turbocharge your portfolio management and risk assessment, a crucial step on the road to becoming a millionaire. With ChatGPT's support, you'll have a comprehensive understanding of your portfolio's performance, enabling you to make informed decisions and maximize your returns. ChatGPT can help you delve into the intricacies of portfolio returns, volatility, and risk-adjusted performance metrics. By comparing these metrics to relevant benchmarks, you'll have a clearer picture of your portfolio's effectiveness and areas that need improvement. This valuable insight will guide you in making strategic adjustments, ensuring that you're always on the path to financial success.

Risk assessment is another area where ChatGPT shines. The AI can analyze correlations between different assets and estimate potential losses during market downturns, providing you with a comprehensive risk profile. This information empowers you to make data-driven adjustments to your portfolio, optimizing it for enhanced returns and reduced risk.

You can ask, "How can ChatGPT help me monitor and evaluate my portfolio's performance, including returns, volatility, and risk-adjusted metrics?" or "What insights can ChatGPT provide to help me identify areas for improvement in my portfolio?"

By leveraging ChatGPT's support in portfolio management and risk assessment, you'll be well-equipped to make smarter investment decisions and unlock the true potential of your wealth-building journey.

Adjusting your investment strategy based on AI-driven insights

As market conditions and personal financial goals evolve, it's crucial to adapt your investment strategy accordingly. ChatGPT can provide AI-driven insights to help investors identify new opportunities, recognize market trends, and assess potential risks.

By continually analyzing market data and adjusting investment recommendations, ChatGPT can enable investors to stay ahead of the curve and make proactive decisions that align with their financial objectives. This dynamic approach to investment management, powered by AI, can ultimately lead to higher profits and long-term financial success.

A great prompt to use is, "How can ChatGPT's AI-driven insights help me adapt my investment strategy as market conditions and personal financial goals evolve?" or "What specific recommendations can ChatGPT provide to help me identify new opportunities, recognize market trends, and assess potential risks?"

Embrace the millionaire mindset by harnessing the power of ChatGPT to fine-tune your investment strategy as market conditions and personal financial goals change. With AI-driven insights at your fingertips, you'll be well-equipped to identify new opportunities, recognize market trends, and assess potential risks, keeping you ahead of the game in the world of investing.

ChatGPT's continuous analysis of market data and investment recommendations will empower you to make proactive decisions that align with your financial objectives. Imagine having a personal financial advisor that never sleeps, always staying on top of market shifts and trends, giving you the edge, you need to maximize your profits.

You can use a prompt such as, "How can I leverage ChatGPT's continuous analysis of market data to make proactive investment decisions that align with my financial objectives?" or "What are some examples of investment strategy adjustments I can make based on ChatGPT's insights to maximize profits and achieve long-term financial success?"

This dynamic approach to investment management, powered by AI, can lead to higher profits and long-term financial success. By adapting your strategy based on ChatGPT's insights, you'll be better prepared to seize opportunities and mitigate risks, propelling you toward your millionaire dreams.

Cryptocurrency and Alt Coin Analysis

Understanding the cryptocurrency market with AI-generated insights

Cryptocurrencies have become a popular alternative investment, but their volatile nature can make it challenging to navigate the market. ChatGPT can help investors better understand the cryptocurrency landscape by providing AI-generated insights based on market trends, historical price data, and sentiment analysis.

These insights can aid investors in identifying potential investment opportunities and making informed decisions about their cryptocurrency holdings. By leveraging ChatGPT's data-driven analysis, investors can gain a more profound understanding of the crypto market, leading to more profitable investment choices.

Ask ChatGPT to help by using the prompt, "How can ChatGPT provide AI-generated insights to help me better understand the cryptocurrency market and its trends?" or "How can I use Google Sheets and a crypto price API to analyze and identify potential cryptocurrency investment opportunities?"

Navigating the volatile cryptocurrency market can be a daunting task, but with ChatGPT's AI-generated insights, you can sail the seas of digital assets like a seasoned captain. By providing data-driven analysis on market trends, historical price data, and sentiment analysis, ChatGPT can help you chart a course toward crypto success.

Imagine being able to pinpoint potential investment opportunities and make informed decisions about your cryptocurrency holdings with confidence. By leveraging ChatGPT's expertise, you can gain a deeper understanding of the crypto market and transform that knowledge into more profitable investment choices, boosting your chances of reaching the heights of other millionaires.

Get help on this with, "What are a list of reliable crypto currency websites where I can get up to date news from?" or "What types of data does ChatGPT analyze to help me identify potential cryptocurrency investment opportunities?"

With ChatGPT, you'll never feel lost in the vast ocean of cryptocurrencies, as this AI-powered tool acts as your personal compass, guiding you through the choppy waters of digital asset investing. Embrace the excitement and harness the power of AI to steer your crypto journey toward wealth and prosperity.

Evaluating ICOs, DeFi projects, and NFTs using ChatGPT

Initial coin offerings (ICOs), decentralized finance (DeFi) projects, and non-fungible tokens (NFTs) are emerging investment opportunities in the world of digital assets. ChatGPT can assist investors in evaluating these opportunities by analyzing whitepapers, project roadmaps, and team credentials.

By providing an objective assessment of these factors, ChatGPT can help investors determine the potential risks and rewards associated with these investments. This AI-powered evaluation can support investors in making more informed decisions and capitalizing on promising opportunities in the rapidly evolving digital asset landscape.

You can use the prompt, "How can ChatGPT help me analyze ICOs, DeFi projects, and NFTs to make better investment decisions?" or "What factors does ChatGPT consider when evaluating the potential risks and rewards of investing in ICOs, DeFi projects, and NFTs?"

Initial coin offerings (ICOs), decentralized finance (DeFi) projects, and non-fungible tokens (NFTs) can be potential goldmines for investors seeking to become millionaires. ChatGPT is your trusty sidekick, helping you evaluate these opportunities by meticulously analyzing whitepapers, project roadmaps, and team credentials. Think of ChatGPT as your personal investment detective, providing an objective assessment of these factors to help you determine the potential risks and rewards associated with these investments. This AI-powered evaluation is like having a crystal ball that offers insights into the rapidly evolving digital asset landscape.

You can ask, "How can ChatGPT's AI-powered evaluation of ICOs, DeFi projects, and NFTs assist me in identifying promising investment opportunities?" or "Give me a list of the websites showing the best times to buy bitcoins over the past 3 years "

Armed with the knowledge and understanding provided by ChatGPT, you can make more informed decisions and capitalize on promising opportunities in ICOs, DeFi projects, and NFTs. With this invaluable tool in your arsenal, you'll be well on your way to unearthing those hidden gems that can propel you towards the investor status you always dreamt of.

Diversifying your investments with AI-assisted alternative asset analysis

Alternative investments, such as real estate, commodities, and private equity, can offer portfolio diversification and help improve risk-adjusted returns. ChatGPT can support investors in evaluating these alternative assets by providing AI-assisted analysis of factors like historical performance, market conditions, and asset correlations.

By leveraging ChatGPT's insights, investors can make better-informed decisions about which alternative investments to include in their portfolios, enhancing overall portfolio diversification and potentially boosting returns.

Use an amazing prompt such as, "How can ChatGPT help me evaluate alternative investments like real estate, commodities, and private equity?" or "What factors should I consider when diversifying my portfolio with alternative investments, and how can ChatGPT assist with this process?"

Alternative investments, such as real estate, commodities, and private equity, can be the key to unlocking vast wealth and achieving millionaire status. With ChatGPT's support, you can delve into the world of alternative assets and make better-informed decisions that could potentially boost your returns. ChatGPT becomes your personal financial analyst, providing AI-assisted analysis of factors like historical performance, market conditions, and asset correlations. This valuable information can help you determine which alternative investments to include in your portfolio, leading to enhanced diversification and improved risk-adjusted returns.

A great prompt is, "How can AI-assisted analysis of alternative assets lead to improved risk-adjusted returns?" or "What are some examples of successful alternative investments that ChatGPT has helped identify?"

Imagine having the power to identify lucrative alternative investments before they become mainstream, all with the help of ChatGPT. By leveraging this cutting-edge AI technology, you'll be one step ahead in the game, making intelligent investment decisions that could pave the way to your millionaire dreams.

Staying Informed and Adapting to the Market

Monitoring market news and trends with AI-generated summaries

Staying informed about market news and trends is crucial for making sound investment decisions. ChatGPT can help investors stay up to date by generating concise summaries of relevant news articles, financial reports, and industry updates.

By providing easily digestible information, ChatGPT enables investors to quickly grasp the most important developments in the market. This AI-powered assistance allows investors to save time and focus on making informed decisions, ultimately leading to more profitable investment outcomes.

Just try asking, "How can ChatGPT help me stay informed about market news and trends to make better investment decisions?" or "What types of news and reports can ChatGPT analyze to generate concise summaries for investors?"

In the fast-paced world of investing, millionaires are made by staying ahead of the curve, leveraging cutting-edge tools to make informed decisions. ChatGPT is the ultimate sidekick for investors striving for the height of financial freedom, providing concise summaries of the most relevant market news, financial reports, and industry updates. With ChatGPT's AI-generated summaries, you'll never miss a beat. Instead of sifting through countless articles and reports, you can focus on using these condensed insights to make more profitable investment decisions. This powerful AI tool enables you to seize lucrative opportunities, adapt your investment strategy, and thrive in an ever-changing market.

You can use a prompt such as, "What is the best dates to buy stocks on typically the times that people go on holidays?" or "What types of news and reports are best to find out the behind the headlines story?"

Picture yourself as a market-savvy investor, always one step ahead of the competition, thanks to ChatGPT's ability to keep you informed about the latest developments. This invaluable advantage will help you navigate the market with confidence and precision, ultimately contributing to your millionaire journey.

Reacting to market changes using ChatGPT's real-time insights

Market conditions can change rapidly, and being able to react swiftly can be the key to successful investing. ChatGPT can provide real-time insights by analyzing market data, social media sentiment, and other relevant factors.

These AI-generated insights can help investors identify emerging trends, potential risks, and investment opportunities as they arise. By incorporating ChatGPT's real-time analysis into their decision-making process, investors can stay ahead of market shifts and make more timely and informed decisions.

What you can easily ask is, "How does ChatGPT provide real-time insights by analyzing market data, social media sentiment, and other factors?" or "How can using ChatGPT's real-time insights help me stay ahead of market shifts and make better investment decisions?"

In the race to become a millionaire, staying on top of real-time market changes is essential. ChatGPT is a game-changer, providing instant insights by analyzing market data, social media sentiment, and other crucial factors. With this powerful AI tool at your disposal, you can act swiftly and decisively, capturing opportunities that others may miss.

Imagine the possibilities that ChatGPT's real-time analysis unlocks for investors. Spotting emerging trends before the masses, detecting potential risks before they materialize, and capitalizing on lucrative investment opportunities as they arise. These AI-generated insights will give you the edge needed to excel in the highly competitive world of investing.

To help with this, ask, "Give me some real time market news and updates from reliable sources on the web in [your year]" or "How can I incorporate ChatGPT's real-time analysis into my decision-making process to improve my investment strategy?"

Incorporating ChatGPT's real-time analysis into your decision-making process is like having an invaluable, highly efficient team of analysts working around the clock. This invaluable resource allows you to adapt your investment strategy and react to market shifts, ensuring that you stay ahead of the curve in your journey to millionaire investor status.

Continuously refining your investment strategy through AI-enhanced learning

An effective investment strategy requires continuous refinement based on new information and changing market conditions. ChatGPT can support investors in this process by providing AI-enhanced learning capabilities.

By analyzing historical investment performance, market data, and investor behavior, ChatGPT can help identify areas for improvement in an investor's strategy. This AI-driven feedback enables investors to make data-driven adjustments to their investment approach, resulting in a more optimized and profitable strategy over time.

You can ask, "How can ChatGPT analyze historical investment performance, market data, and investor behavior to help me refine my investment strategy?" or "What are some examples of AI-enhanced learning capabilities that ChatGPT provides to support investors in optimizing their investment strategies?"

A millionaire investor's journey is marked by the relentless pursuit of an optimized investment strategy, and ChatGPT is the key ingredient to achieving this. By offering AI-enhanced learning capabilities, ChatGPT can turn your investment approach into a well-oiled, profit-generating machine. Imagine the power of harnessing ChatGPT to analyze historical investment performance, market data, and investor behavior. This AI-driven analysis can uncover hidden patterns and opportunities, pinpointing areas where your investment strategy can be improved. With this valuable feedback, you can make data-driven adjustments, finetuning your approach for maximum profitability.

A great prompt to use is, "What are some practical ways to implement the AI-driven feedback provided by ChatGPT in order to adjust my investment approach?" "How can I use ChatGPT's AI-enhanced learning to identify hidden patterns and opportunities in the market?"

The continuous refinement provided by ChatGPT is like having a personal investment coach that never sleeps, constantly adapting your strategy to stay ahead of the competition. This AI-enhanced learning will give you the edge needed to conquer the market and secure your place among the millionaires.

Conclusion

In conclusion, this book has equipped you with ten innovative money-making ideas that leverage the power of ChatGPT to help you achieve your financial goals. By understanding the potential of AI in various fields, such as content creation, online courses, e-commerce, ghostwriting, copywriting, virtual assistance, and investment analysis, you have unlocked new opportunities to generate income and diversify your revenue streams.

As you embark on this exciting journey, keep in mind that the key to success lies in acting and implementing the strategies outlined in each chapter. Start by choosing the ideas that resonate most with your skills, interests, and goals. Then, develop a plan and commit to making consistent progress. With dedication, perseverance, and the support of ChatGPT as your AI-powered ally, you will be well on your way to creating a thriving, profitable venture.

Throughout this process, it's essential to stay informed about the latest advancements in AI and continually refine your approach based on new insights and developments. Embrace a growth mindset and invest in your learning and personal development, as this will pay dividends in your financial success.

Lastly, remember that the journey to financial success is not a linear one, and you may encounter challenges along the way. Embrace these setbacks as learning opportunities and use them to strengthen your resolve and adapt your strategies. With the right mindset, the invaluable support of ChatGPT, and a commitment to continuous improvement, there is no doubt that financial success is within your reach.

Now, it's time to take the first step and make your financial dreams a reality. Implement the strategies you've learned in this book, watch your income soar, and celebrate the achievements that come with unlocking the incredible potential of AI-enhanced money-making opportunities. Good luck and happy earnings!

Bonus Chapter

The Everyday Ai

As the field of artificial intelligence (AI) continues to progress and diversify at an extraordinary pace, it is increasingly influencing various aspects of our lives. The rapid advancements in natural language processing, computer vision, and deep learning are transforming industries and paving the way for groundbreaking innovations.

In this bonus chapter, we will delve into the future of AI by examining the implications of AI-driven platforms like Open AI Codex and exploring other remarkable potential applications of AI across various domains.

AI in Healthcare: Transforming Diagnosis and Treatment

The future of AI in healthcare is promising, with the potential to revolutionize the way medical professionals diagnose and treat patients. AI algorithms can analyze large volumes of data, identifying patterns and trends that may be difficult for human experts to discern. This capability enables AI to assist in early disease detection, more accurate diagnoses, personalized treatment plans, and even the development of new drugs. As AI continues to advance, we can expect its role in healthcare to expand, improving patient outcomes and optimizing healthcare delivery.

AI in Education: Enhancing Learning Experiences

AI holds immense potential for transforming the education sector by providing personalized learning experiences, automating administrative tasks, and offering insights into student performance. AI-powered learning platforms can adapt to individual students' needs, delivering tailored content that optimizes their learning experience. In the future, AI could play a significant role in democratizing education by making high-quality, personalized learning accessible to students across the globe, regardless of their socioeconomic background.

Open AI Codex: Revolutionizing Programming

Open AI Codex is an AI model that can understand, interpret, and generate code in multiple programming languages. It has the potential to significantly impact the programming landscape by offering an AI-assisted coding experience for developers. Codex is trained on a vast repository of publicly available code, allowing it to provide context-aware suggestions, autocomplete code, and even create entirely new functions based on user inputs.

As AI progresses, we can anticipate that platforms like Open AI Codex will become increasingly sophisticated and adaptive, automating routine tasks, and enhancing the development process. This will ultimately enable developers to focus on solving complex problems and fostering innovation.

Revolutionizing the Programming Landscape

The introduction of AI-powered coding assistants like Copilot is set to transform the programming landscape dramatically. By leveraging advanced AI algorithms, these tools can significantly enhance the development process and enable programmers to accomplish more in less time. In this section, we will discuss three key features of Copilot and explore how they will revolutionize the way we program.

Context-Aware Code Suggestions

One of the most remarkable features of Copilot is its ability to provide context-aware code suggestions. Trained on an extensive database of publicly available code, Copilot can understand the intent behind user input and offer relevant code snippets or even entire functions based on the context. This feature can save developers time by reducing the need to search for code samples or reinvent the wheel for common tasks.

As AI algorithms become more sophisticated, we can expect even more accurate and relevant code suggestions, helping developers tackle complex challenges more efficiently and effectively.

Accelerated Learning and Knowledge Transfer

Copilot's AI-assisted coding capabilities can also serve as a valuable learning tool for both new and experienced developers. By providing real-time code suggestions, Copilot can help programmers understand best practices, discover new techniques, and learn different programming languages more quickly. This accelerated learning and knowledge transfer can empower developers to expand their skill sets and stay competitive in an ever-evolving industry.

As AI becomes more advanced, it will likely facilitate even more efficient knowledge transfer, enabling developers to adapt to new languages, frameworks, and tools with ease.

Improved Code Quality and Reduced Errors

Another significant benefit of using Copilot is its potential to improve code quality and reduce errors. By offering context-aware suggestions and adhering to best practices, Copilot can help developers avoid common pitfalls and write more efficient, robust code. Additionally, AI algorithms can be trained to identify potential security vulnerabilities and suggest appropriate measures to mitigate them.

In the future, AI-powered coding assistants like Copilot may become even more adept at detecting and preventing errors, ensuring that the code we write is more reliable and secure.

Enhanced Collaboration and Code Review

Copilot and similar AI tools can also play a role in enhancing collaboration and code review processes. By providing AI-generated insights into the code's structure, performance, and potential issues, these tools can help development teams work more effectively and collaboratively. This can result in faster iteration cycles, more efficient debugging, and ultimately, better software products.

As AI continues to advance, we can anticipate even more effective collaboration and code review tools that streamline the software development process.

The Future of AI in Graphics

The rapid advancement of artificial intelligence is transforming the graphics industry, driving innovation, and creating new opportunities for artists, designers, and content creators. In this section, we will discuss the future of AI in graphics, focusing on three groundbreaking features and software packages that are set to reshape the way we create and consume visual content.

Open Ai's DALL-E: Next-Generation Image Synthesis

DALL-E, an AI model developed by Open AI, is a groundbreaking technology that can generate original images from textual descriptions. By combining the power of natural language understanding and advanced image synthesis algorithms, DALL-E can create stunning, high-quality visuals based on user inputs.

The future of DALL-E promises even greater capabilities in image synthesis, allowing for more accurate and detailed image generation from increasingly complex textual descriptions. As technology advances, we can expect DALL-E to become an indispensable tool for artists, designers, and content creators, enabling them to bring their ideas to life with unprecedented ease and precision.

AI-Driven 3D Modeling and Animation

The integration of AI into 3D modeling and animation software packages is set to revolutionize the way we create and interact with digital environments. AI algorithms can be used to automate repetitive tasks, such as generating realistic textures, optimizing geometry, or even creating entire scenes based on simple user inputs.

One such example is NVIDIA's GANverse3D, which can transform 2D images into 3D models using generative adversarial networks (GANs). As AI algorithms continue to evolve, we can expect even more powerful 3D modeling and animation tools that streamline the creative process and unlock new possibilities in virtual and augmented reality, gaming, and digital media production.

AI-Assisted Video Editing and Visual Effects

The integration of AI into video editing and visual effects software is another exciting development in the graphics industry. AI-driven tools can automate time-consuming tasks like rotoscoping, object tracking, and color grading, allowing video editors and visual effects artists to focus on the creative aspects of their work.

For example, Adobe's Sensei AI technology is already being used to power various features in their Creative Cloud suite, including content-aware fill, automatic masking, and scene re-lighting. As AI algorithms become more advanced, we can anticipate even more innovative video editing and visual effects tools that significantly enhance the creative process and open new possibilities for storytelling and visual communication.

In conclusion, this bonus chapter has provided a glimpse into the exciting future of artificial intelligence, with a focus on the Copilot development environment and the transformative potential of AI in graphics and design. As we continue to push the boundaries of AI capabilities, we can expect even more groundbreaking innovations and applications across various industries. The future holds immense promise, with AI technology poised to revolutionize how we work, create, and communicate. So, stay curious, keep learning, and be prepared to embrace the incredible opportunities that AI will bring in the years to come. The journey has only just begun, and the possibilities are truly limitless.

Resources

https://www.deeplearning.ai/

You can take the very latest course for free in ChatGPT Prompt Engineering. It is endorsed and developed with approval from Open AI. Hurry though, it might not be free forever.

https://www.midjourney.com/

The world's best software for creating AI images for your own personal or business use. You can try several free prompts to generate anything from your imagination.

https://prompts.chat/

An online guide to many different prompts that you can use and have been tested by users around the world. If you are new to prompts and want more experience with them, this resource is for you.

https://durable.co/

Build a marketing website with the help of AI in just a few minutes. Take your site and customize it to how you want.

https://www.blackhatworld.com/

The world's leading forum for money making online, where many users are utilizing ChatGPT and discussing how they are using it to make an income from various revenue channels.

Don't miss out!

Visit the website below and you can sign up to receive emails whenever C Edmiston publishes a new book. There's no charge and no obligation.

https://books2read.com/r/B-A-JISY-AWTJC

BOOKS 2 READ

Connecting independent readers to independent writers.